COMMUNICATING
QUANTITIES

Communicating Quantities

A Psychological Perspective

Linda M. Moxey

and

Anthony J. Sanford

Human Communication Research Centre
Department of Psychology
University of Glasgow, Glasgow, UK

LAWRENCE ERLBAUM ASSOCIATES, PUBLISHERS
Hove (UK)   Hillsdale (USA)

Lawrence Erlbaum Associates Ltd., Publishers
27 Palmeira Mansions
Church Road
Hove
East Sussex, BN3 2FA
UK

British Library Cataloguing in Publication Data

Moxey, Linda M.
   Communicating Quantities: Psychological
   Perspective. (Essays in Cognitive
   Psychology Series, ISSN 0959-4779)
   I. Title II. Sanford, Anthony J.
   III. Series
   153.7

ISBN 0-86377-225-0

Printed and bound in the United Kingdom by BPCC Wheatons Ltd., Exeter

Dedicated to Iain and Bridget

Contents

Preface

Natural language quantifiers are ubiquitous in languages and acts of communication. Despite this fact, they have received relatively little systematic attention from psychologists, although, in recent years at least, logicians of a linguistic persuasion have been extremely active in exploring their semantic description as a general problem. In psychology, there have been two main traditions of work. Perhaps best known is work on reasoning with quantifiers, especially within the framework of the syllogism. As a result of theory-building in this area, quantifiers have become centrally involved in Johnson-Laird's theory of mental models (Johnson-Laird, 1983) and in his general ideas about deduction (Johnson-Laird & Byrne, 1991). But the quantifiers considered in these treatments, and those who dispute the arguments about mental models, are extremely restricted. In the main, they are restricted to the classical quantifiers that have been analysed as the logical quantifiers $\forall$ and $\exists$. There are many other natural language quantifiers (many, few, etc.) that are commonplace, yet they have received attention from only a very limited perspective in psychology.

This limited perspective is concerned with such issues as *how many is many, how many is few*, and for related expressions, *how often is seldom,* and *how probable is likely*. We term this the psychometric approach. It grew up in a practical tradition rather than in a theoretical one, and can be said, without demeaning the interesting work which has been done, to be largely atheoretical. (It might be fairer to call it *extratheoretical*, as it has been mostly concerned with practical matters). But work in this tradition has not been shy of including the vasticum of expressions characteristic of what occurs in natural language. It is quite possible to put a number on *many* or *a large amount* given an appropriate context, and such numbers have practical implications in a variety of settings. But there are problems with this approach: There is no demonstration that listeners translate numbers onto internal scales. If they do, the evidence we review in Chapters 1 and 2 certainly suggests that such scales are relatively crude affairs. One of the most obvious outcomes of the psychometric approach is that quantifiers overlap enormously when projected onto any simple numerical scale. In this event, why should there be quite so many expressions available to us to answer questions of *how many, how much,* and, analogously, *how often?*

The answer is obviously to be found in the semantic and communicative properties of the expressions. In general, those psychologists who have thought about nonstandard quantifiers have not paid much attention to work in pragmatics and semantics that might be helpful in understanding the mental processes surrounding quantifier usage. Part of our task is to review some of this work with an eye to seeing how it might assist the psychologists' quest. Work in pragmatics clearly illustrates both the importance of being sufficiently specific in answering *how many* questions, but not overspecific or overaccurate, and the importance of consideration of meaning beyond truth conditions in a more general way. Work in semantics since the late 1970s has begun to show how natural language quantifiers are but a small subset of the mathematical possibilities for quantifiers, thus providing arguments about how natural languages are restricted in relation to the generalised notion of a language. This approach has proved to be very productive in the understanding of a whole range of phenomena, including aspects of negativity, which is a pervasive factor in the analysis of quantifiers. Because our approach is psychological, we have not described this work in detail, although we have made use of some of its results, and, perhaps more important, provided a way of integrating psychological phenomena with the way intuitive tests based on semantic theory might work.

At the very least, our intention is to bring some of the nonpsychological work into psychological discussion of nonstandard quantifiers. Beyond this, we offer some original studies of a psychological nature which we hope will restore the balance by moving the focus of interest away from the psychometric approach. But our ultimate hope is that some of the work described here may contribute to an interdisciplinary approach to natural language quantifiers. Although the conditions of use of quantifiers are bound to be describable in a formalism, we believe that any realistic answer to the question of which quantifier a speaker should use when, and how it will be interpreted, ultimately requires the kind of psychological data and theory which we outline here.

Those of a formal persuasion will doubtlessly find some of what we have to say perhaps a little casual. But to any reader who has this orientation, we must point out that while our concern is not to vindicate the application of any particular (formal) semantic theory, we are in part motivated by a philosophy nicely stated by Barwise and Cooper (1981) in their seminal paper on how well natural language quantifiers might be described within a mathematical formulation of possible quantifiers, generalised quantifier theory. The task was to establish whether formal (mathematical) properties of an idealised quantifier theory could be found in the full variety of natural language quantifiers. Of the relation of formal treatments to judgements of language, Barwise and Cooper (1981, pp. 201–202) said:

> While it is seldom made explicit, it is sometimes assumed that there is some system of axioms and rules of logic engraved on stone tablets—that an inference in natural language is valid only if it can be formalised by means of these axioms and rules. In actuality, the situation is quite the reverse. The native speaker's judgements as to whether a certain inference is correct, whether the truth of the hypothesis implies the truth of the conclusion, is primary evidence for a semantic theory in just the way that grammaticality judgements are used as primary evidence for a syntactic theory.

For the psychologist, one step further may be taken. That is that judgements about statements in a language are considered to be acts of information processing (like any other kind of decision-making) rather than being a retrieval of some piece of platonic knowledge. This represents the authors' orientation to the whole issue of linguistic acceptability.

This book is the result of a research programme, which began with Linda Moxey's PhD work (Moxey, 1986), supported by the ESRC. Linda Moxey thanks the British Academy for a postdoctoral research fellowship that allowed the work to continue, and Tony Sanford thanks ESRC for support. Over the last few years, a number of colleagues and students have joined us in parts of the project, the fruit of which is cited in this book. In Glasgow, we owe a debt to Stephen Barton, Simon Garrod, Gillian Grant, Marie McGinley, and Kevin Patterson. The research benefited greatly from discussions within the Semantic Processing Working Group of the Human Communication Research Centre, which included some of the people mentioned above, but also Jonathan Broadbent, Robin Cooper, Martin Emms, Elisabet Engdahl, Kate Gillen, and Rosemary Stevenson. Outside the local intellectual environment, there are many people to thank for their help and criticism, and we would like to mention especially Pieter Seuren who stimulated our efforts to bring formal and psychological approaches to meaning into contact. In various ways Dave Farwell, Dennis Hilton, Phil Johnson-Laird, and Steve Newstead also had a major impact on the development of this book.

Linda Moxey
Tony Sanford
Glasgow, 1992

CHAPTER ONE

Introduction

INTRODUCTION

Words and expressions that appear to be vague descriptions of quantity, frequency, and probability permeate our language. News reports are full of vague statements that we as listeners seem to find easy to understand. For instance: "Many of the soldiers have not eaten for several days"; "A few of the Conservative backbenchers complained about the Poll tax"; "Opinion polls often show increased support for the government during war time". Such statements are commonplace, yet it is difficult to give any formal, precise statement of their exact meaning. The first statement may be quite appropriate if 20% of the soldiers have not eaten for three days, but it will also be true if 60% of them have not eaten for five days; the second could be true if 3 Members of Parliament complained or if 30 did, and so on.

The quantity-denoting expressions used in these examples are but a few of a large set of expressions that convey quantitative information about the world, albeit vaguely or imprecisely. They are just as likely to be found in scientific textbooks as in the deliberately obfuscated utterances of politicians, or in ordinary conversation. For the cognitive psychologist, they present an interesting set of problems. Are they merely vague expressions second best to actual numerical values that a speaker may not be too sure about? Or do they convey something quite different, and if so, what? Psychologists have certainly paid considerable attention to the relation of such expressions to numerical scales, yielding a considerable number of papers, including ones with such nicely illustrative titles as *Sometimes frequently means seldom* ... (Pepper & Prytulak, 1974), *How often is often?* (Hakel, 1969) for the frequency domain, and *How probable is probable?* ... (Beyth-Marom, 1982) for the probability domain. For quantifiers, the same amusing questions can be posed. In Chapter 2, we shall review the evidence relating to this approach more fully.

Some Uses of the Scaling Approach

Treating quantifying expressions as vaguely denoting quantities is an obvious thing to do.[1] And it has its uses. For instance, recent interest in the development of expert systems that are meant to mimic expert decision-maker's activities often have to confront problems of uncertainty and quantification (see, e.g., D. Clark, 1990, for a recent review). The problem stems from the fact that experts themselves typically produce decision-making protocols that contain information of an apparently probabilistic kind, for instance, *"given symptoms X and Y, then it is possible/likely that disease X is present"*. Such statements suggest a strategy of translating the vague terms into probabilities, or distributions of possible values, and adopting a numerical approach to handling these values within an expert system. Examples of numerical approaches include Bayesian and fuzzy set approaches (D. Clark, 1990). Research aimed directly at the association between probability terms and numerical scales, such as probability distributions, does not necessarily result from the practical problems of those trying to extract information from experts. Nevertheless, it is clear that the scaling philosophy has a practical application in this area. We shall examine this point in more detail in Chapter 2.

An even earlier applied problem making use of the scale approach is the design of psychometric questionnaires. A widely used technique in psychometrics is to present people with some description, and have them check one of a set of optional responses. These options often use vague quantifiers or frequency adverbs rather than numbers or percentages. For instance:

I have gloomy thoughts:
☐ Never ☐ rarely ☐ sometimes ☐ often ☐ all of the time
(tick one)

In the face of this, a considerable amount of research has gone into determining the "precise" meaning of such expressions (reviewed in Chapter 2). One idea is that if such expressions are to be useful in a psychometric context, then they should have similar meanings for all people, and have consistent meanings for a given person (where the notion of meaning is restricted to numerical denotation). Another psychometric issue has been the search for a maximally discriminating set of expressions to cover the complete underlying scale. Suppose that the scale underlying the expressions in the aforementioned example above is 0–100. Do the five items presented divide the scale up into five equal regions (i.e. do they achieve interval scaling)? If not, which expressions are optimal to give a maximally discriminating scale? How many equal-sized regions are possible? These are the kinds of questions which underlie the psychometric approach; illustrative work includes Beyth-Marom (1982) on probability terms, and Bass, Cascio, and O'Connor (1974) and Hartley, Trueman, and Rogers (1984) on quantifiers and frequency adjectives.

The Unidimensionality Assumption

Because of the concentration of effort by psychologists on expression-to-number mapping, there may be a tendency to suppose that the meanings of quantifiers are adequately captured within this framework. Such a view has been termed a unidimensional framework (D. Clark, 1990). Typical evidence consistent with such a point of view has been obtained with probability terms by Reyna (1981), who used sorting, ranking, and magnitude estimation as scaling methods to determine subjective dimensionality. She concluded that the expressions are "internally represented in terms of degrees along a unidimensional scale of quantification" (p. 649). However, such a pattern of results does not really prove the unidimensionality hypothesis, because there may be other aspects of the meaning of the expressions that are not predicted by a unidimensional account. Furthermore, because subjects *can* scale items does not mean that the representations enabling this themselves amount to a single dimension.

First, the superficial plausibility of the scale-mapping hypothesis depends critically on what expressions we are considering. For example, those reflecting degree of likelihood, or probability, like *a good chance*, *probable*, etc., seem to fit this scheme naturally. But there are certain other expressions that do not fit so readily. For example, if we are told that during the early military strikes of the Gulf War "*a significant number* of SCUD missiles were disarmed", just what does this mean? One possibility is that it is so vague as to be meaningless. But this does not seem to be a completely fair appraisal, as it is clearly different from saying *an insignificant number*. It seems to mean something like, *a number of missiles were disarmed that is big enough to count as a satisfactory outcome given some level of expectation of what is satisfactory*. In short, it seems to depend on a value judgement, the acceptability of which will be a function of how much the listener believes the speaker to know. Such attempted paraphrases simply serve to illustrate how difficult it is to establish just what such a statement might mean, however. To understand such statements further, we have to look into more pragmatic aspects of usage. The point here is to illustrate how difficult the idea of a unidimensional description of the meanings of quantity expressions might turn out to be in practice.

There are circumstances where a natural language expression might be better than an exact number, because the expression conveys extra information not conveyed by its numerical denotation. For instance, if I want to book a seat on a train in the near future, and I telephone to check availability, I do not want to be told that 20% of the seats are reserved, or even that there are 95 seats left. I want to know whether there is any hurry to reserve a seat: If the expert tells me that there are *many* seats left (or *plenty* of seats), he is telling me that there are *many* or *plenty* relative to my implicit question regarding reservations. If the expert does not want to commit himself to advising me on whether I should reserve early, but he suspects that I need not, then his use of *many* or *plenty* is fair enough. He is telling me that there is no need to rush provided normal patterns of reservation follow. Note how useless it is to be told that 20% of the seats are left , since this cannot be used unless I happen to know what is normal. So the natural language statement again seems to be a value judgement, and the choice of the expression relies upon the speaker having some idea of what the listener's goals are.

Expressions Considered in this Book

Our discussion up to now has picked out one or two illustrative expressions, covering a number of linguistic categories. The main class that is considered in this monograph is the class of *quantifiers*, which we take to mean expressions that either make assertions about the number of things being talked about, or indicate a subset of some superset. These expressions are concerned with numbers or proportions of *things*, and we shall argue that they can be treated within a uniform account. The expressions already introduced give no real idea of the astonishing variety of ways in which quasi-numerical information may be conveyed. An impression of the variety can be gained from a study carried out by Moxey (1986), in which subjects were asked to describe drawings with different proportions of male and female pin-figures in such a way that a listener could select the correct one from a set. Subjects were not allowed to use numbers or percentages, and so used purely natural language expressions. It is astonishing that no less than 182 different expressions were used given the 825 descriptions produced! It seems reasonable to suppose that this variety of expressions does not correspond to 182 different "percentage points", but rather that many of the expressions must denote effectively identical proportions, or ranges of proportions. This, of course, raises the question of why there is such a great variety.

While in this book we shall concentrate on (amount) quantifiers, another closely related set of expressions is *quantifying adverbs*, such as *often, frequently, rarely*, and so on. These expressions indicate numbers or proportions of occasions on which some event happens. Finally, there are expressions relating to expectation and subjective probability, such as *probable, unlikely, very probable, distinctly possible,* etc. These expressions have been given considerable attention within the scaling framework and we shall describe some of this work. Table 1.1 illustrates some of the expressions that have been used by investigators in various studies, including some of the set produced spontaneously by Moxey's subjects. There is no attempt at classification, the table is merely to show some of the astonishing range of expressions.

Almost all of the expressions in Table 1.1 are vague in that they do not clearly denote a particular amount, proportion, or subjective likelihood, although they may possibly denote ranges of these things. However, there are yet other ways of conveying vague quantitative information in natural language. Apart from explicit words or phrases that serve as quantifiers, discourse is permeated with what might be termed generalisations. These have the appearance of universal statements, but are seldom intended to be understood as such. An example is:

(1) The imperialists use inhuman weapons.

Such a claim made in a propaganda broadcast is likely to mean, more strictly, something like (2):

(2) Some imperialists have occasionally used a few inhuman weapons.

TABLE 1.1

Examples of Expressions Illustrating a Variety of Types

Frequency expressions: Always, very nearly always, very often, a great deal of the time, usually, commonly, frequently, quite often, sometimes, now and then, periodically, occasionally, seldom, rarely, hardly ever.

Probability expressions: Almost certain, highly probable, very likely, a good chance, likely, even odds, somewhat unlikely, doubtful, poor chance, exceedingly unlikely, almost impossible, vanishingly small odds.

Quantifiers: All, not quite all, nearly all, an awful lot, a lot, a comfortable majority, most, many, more than N, less than N, quite a few, quite a lot, several, not a lot, not many, only a few, few, a few, hardly any.

As Abelson and Kanouse (1966) point out, the rhetorical impact of the generalisation form is much better than the quantified form. Clearly, (1) is unlikely to be interpreted as a universal (generic) statement the way the following is:

(3) Birds can fly.

In fact, (1) is vague, and such apparent generalisations turn out to be very context-dependent. For instance, *people buy clothes* is likely to be understood as *most people buy some clothes sometimes*, so a few instances would be enough to make the statement acceptable, whereas *people hate Martians* would only be acceptable if most people hated all Martians. With implicit quantification, then, determination of meaning depends in large measure upon the situation under discussion. This is true of forms other than the generalisation, including forms with well-understood logical properties such as "there are": *There are people who believe that women should not be ordained into the ministry.* Together with explicit vague quantification, generalisations are rife in expository and other types of discourse. How they are understood, and how they are represented in memory for discourse is worthy of consideration.

Quantification within Psychological Models of Text Comprehension

Current psychological models of text comprehension have paid little or no heed to the problem of quantification as outlined earlier. Indeed, outside the psychometric work on scaling, almost all of the psychological work has been concerned with the use of quantifiers within the framework of syllogistic reasoning (e.g. Johnson-Laird, 1983). This may not be surprising for a number of reasons, not the least of which is the broad range of problems that theories have to address. Another reason might well be the logical intractability of many of the most commonplace quantifiers, which makes them difficult to express in tidy and seemingly meaningful formats such as the proposition. There is no explicit treatment of quantification in the theories of Gernsbacher (1990), Kintsch and van Dijk (1978), Sanford and Garrod (1981), and no sign of a discussion of such issues in the new generation of connectionist-inspired models (e.g. Dolan, 1989; Sharkey, 1990).

Johnson-Laird's work deals in the main with the standard quantifiers *all, some, some don't,* and *no(ne)*, which have special properties, as discussed in the next section. His theory of mental models sets out to explain how without recourse to an explicit mental logic, it is possible to carry out valid syllogistic reasoning. His account also allows for predictions to be made regarding the order of difficulty of various syllogisms, and the kinds of errors that subjects produce. Essentially, it is a problem-solving approach. It is of course an open question whether the machinery of mental models as described by Johnson-Laird might underlie the comprehension of discourse containing quantified statements. Certainly, it is rare to find a syllogistic structure in discourse containing quantifiers; more commonly, quantified statements are used simply to depict or assert states of affairs. It might be the case that his scheme is applicable to *reasoning about what was said* in a text that used quantified statements.

The problem still remains to discover how quantified statements in general are understood. In our view, it is necessary to confront the role of background knowledge in interpretation in order to see how quantified statements are understood. Some of the problems with simple accounts of truth conditions as a way of characterising the meaning of quantifiers are illustrated in the next section.

LOGIC-INSPIRED CONSIDERATIONS

The treatment of quantifiers has been and still is a major issue in logic. It is not our intention to try to review even a fraction of this work, for much of it is not relevant to the psychological perspective (at least, not at present). One fundamental distinction we might make is between standard and nonstandard (or nonlogical) quantifiers.

Standard Quantifiers

The "modern perspective" (as Barwise & Cooper, 1981, termed it), in which nonstandard quantifiers were explored with any thoroughness, did not begin until about the mid 1970s. Until then, most of the logical work centred around those natural language quantifiers that appear to have underlying meanings expressible in terms of the logical quantifiers ∀ (the universal) and ∃ (the existential), what McCawley (1981) called the "logician's favourite quantifiers". The universal corresponds to something like *all* in natural language, while the existential corresponds to the state of there *being at least one* (or *there is some X such that...*). Natural language expressions analysed in this way include, most centrally, *all*, *some*, and *no(ne)*. These are the traditional quantifiers used in syllogisms, and reasoning with them in a syllogistic context has been given an extensive psychological analysis by Johnson-Laird (1983). Closely related to *all* are *each* and *every*, which have also been (not uncontentiously) analysed in terms of ∀ and ∃. Similarly, definite expressions like *the cat* can and have been analysed in terms of the logical quantifiers. Quantifiers that can be defined in terms of ∀ and ∃ are sometimes called logical, because their meaning is purportedly not a function of the situation in which they occur (Zwarts, 1991).

Despite the simplicity of analyses in terms of ∀ and ∃, the use of even the standard natural language quantifiers is not adequately covered by such an approach. This problem crops up in a number of ways. First, we do not say *some X* when we *know all X*, although *all X* is not logically ruled out by *some X*. Rather, we would normally use the expression *all X* if that is what we wished to convey. This is an issue of pragmatics, to be discussed shortly. A related point is that the statement *I saw some children at the swings* seems to mean more than *just one*, yet fewer, perhaps, than *many*. In short, *some* cannot be adequately described by ∃ (at least one). These two points make clear the distinction between what is necessarily true (truth-functional semantics), and what is considered to be the case by any reasonable user of the language (pragmatics). In neither case described earlier is it *false* to say that *some* can be equated with ∀ (or ∃), and it is indeed the case that if anything other than that is assumed, then we cannot guarantee the success of simple syllogistic reasoning. Rather than replace truth-functional semantics, pragmatic inference simply supplements it.

Problems arise because of the apparently sloppy use of the terms *all* and *every*. For instance, a teenager may say:

(4) All of the school knows I've broken up with my girlfriend; or
(5) Everybody wears their shirts outside their trousers these days.

We might say that such statements are not literally true: They are exaggerations. In such a case, *all or everybody* still means ∀, and a way is needed to interpret the (pragmatic) impossibility of (4) or (5) being literally true. Normally, one would read these uses as meaning something like *anyone who matters in the school*. It is apparent that the standard formulation could drive the understanding process in these cases. Parallel arguments can be made for *no* and *never*.

Further problems have been recognised by Labov (1985), who points out other uses of *all*. For instance, the following is an adverbial use:

(6) It was all over the neighbourhood.
(7) It all depends.

He suggests that these mean something like *many people knew about it* and *it depends on many things*, and argues that this necessarily requires a loose interpretation of *all*, in which it corresponds to *nearly all*. It is obvious that we cannot identify the conditions in the world necessary to evaluate the truth of this sort of statement within a strict framework.

Another major use of *all* pointed out by Labov is as an intensifier, illustrated by:

(8) He was all worn out.
(9) She was all confused.

He has established that such uses are among the most common uses of *all*. This use might be equated with the notion of "being at the extreme".

Labov and others have argued that in the light of such nonstandard examples (in the sense of not being interpretable through ∀), *all* can either be strict (standard) or lax (interpreted as *nearly all*). Similarly, *none* can be interpreted strictly (~ ∃) or in a lax way (being indistinguishable from *almost none*). The decisions are pragmatic, and therefore a matter for psychological processing models.

There is some interesting psychological work on this problem, which supports the view that it is hard for people to use the strict interpretation of *all* even in a logic-problem setting. Consider the propositions *All A are B*, and *All B are C*. Because transitivity holds over these two, it follows that *All A are C*. In fact, it holds for any length of sequence. But human subjects are not confident about this, and will sometimes assert that e.g. *All A are C* does not follow (Newstead & Griggs, 1984; Newstead, Pollard, & Griggs, 1986). After a distance of 1 step (i.e. *All A are C*), the probability of rejection was 0.11; after 3 steps (i.e. *All A are E*) it was 0.19 (almost 1 in 5). Newstead and Griggs also observed that the pattern of responses to *all* was almost the same as the pattern of responses when *nearly all* is used, suggesting that these two quantifiers were being treated as the same. This is consonant with Labov's conjecture. There is thus strong empirical evidence to show that even the simplest transitive inference with the simplest logical quantifier in the most obviously logical setting produces a weak (nonlogical) interpretation.

Nonstandard and Generalised Quantifiers

The modern period of logical work on quantifiers effectively started with the observation that there are many quantifiers that cannot be defined in terms of (first-order) ∀ and ∃ (see Montague, 1974; Mostowski, 1957, for a discussion of the application to English quantifiers). Quantifiers outside those defineable in terms of ∀ and ∃ are termed generalised quantifiers, and natural language quantifiers appear to be only a subset of those that are mathematically possible. Barwise and Cooper (1981) were the first to attempt to explore systematically those constraints on possible generalised quantifiers that define the set of natural language quantifiers, and more recent work along similar lines comes from Keenan and Stavi (1986) and Westerståhl (1989). We shall return to some of that work at a later point.

Let us term quantifiers that cannot be defined in terms of first-order ∀ and ∃ *nonstandard*. The majority of the expressions with which we deal here are nonstandard, and have the property of being context-dependent; that is, certain of the inferences that the quantifiers license are dependent upon the things and situations under discussion, which is a problem for defining their truth conditions (which is why they are also sometimes called nonlogical).

Consider the behaviour of the standard quantifier *some*:

(10)   All Quakers are Christians.
      Some Quakers don't go to church.
      Therefore, some Christians don't go to church.

This follows because *some* can be taken to mean *at least one, regardless of context*. But the following fails to behave in the same way:

(11)   All Quakers are Christians.
      Many Quakers don't go to church.
      Therefore, many Christians don't go to church.

The failure appears to be because the number of Quakers is small relative to the number of Christians. And this is a problem for the treatment of *many* in the traditional logical framework, as it means that set size has an effect on the truth or falsity of inferences, and set size can only be known empirically. If we think of *many* as defined by some critical minimum number, then that number will have to depend on set size. This and related problems have been noted and discussed in an early piece of work on nonstandard quantifiers reported by Altham (1971). Among other things he noted the nonequivalence of the following pair:

(12)   Many Quakers are teetotallers.
(12′) Many teetotallers are Quakers.

In complete contrast, the following are equivalent from a truth-functional point of view:[2]

(13)   Some Quakers are teetotallers.
(13′) Some teetotallers are Quakers.

Altham's solution is motivated again by considerations of set size. He introduces a notion of index that captures these set-size effects, arguing that only in the case where the critical number for *many* to apply is the same in both instances does *many A are B* imply *many B are A*. He argued that if one critical value is large and the other small, then the direction of inference that is allowed is from large to small. Thus, (12) follows from

(12′), but not vice versa. Such an analysis again underlines the point that to evaluate the truth of an assertion about a quantified statement containing the term *many*, empirical knowledge has to be imported.

As a final example, note that the following statement is perfectly acceptable to a normal user of English:

(14) There are many severe schizophrenics, but nearly everybody is not severely schizophrenic.

A system in which *many* and *nearly all* are defined in terms of some criterion number cannot possibly allow the acceptance of such a sentence as a well-formed proposition. Yet to the human user, it might be understood as something like: Even a very small proportion of people being schizophrenic counts as many (perhaps because it is so undesirable for there to be any); but a very small proportion of the population being schizophrenic means that nearly everyone is not schizophrenic.

Altham's work was an attempt to capture the meaning of *many* and *nearly all* in terms of a minimum number. When this is done, acceptable propositions like (14) are ruled out, while unacceptable equivalences like (12) are acceptable. Formal accounts can thus be made and evaluated against the performance of language users. If there is a discrepancy, then one could say either that the formalism is not a correct characterisation, or that it is correct, but some extra factors have to be taken into account to fill the gap between performance of the formalism and performance of language users. This is a serious issue; in considering why there was a clash between his formulation and what users would accept, Altham suggested that in common usage, the quantifiers in question are used in a "casual" way, suggesting that "One tendency is to say that there are *many* when there are just *a lot* in some vague sense, and to say that *nearly all* have some property when *an overwhelmingly high proportion* have this property". Such a notion of sloppiness in humans arises because of a belief that a logical model captures the "real" semantics of the expressions, and that performance may "deviate" from this ideal. This is a debatable assumption, to say the least, rather like the view that natural language deviates from true grammar. In fact, what it amounts to is saying that within a limited framework, rules hold that may not hold in a broader communicative framework. This may or may not be an interesting observation, but it is certainly different from the view that human reason somehow misuses the real meanings of expressions.[3] An equally debatable assumption is that *a lot* and *an overwhelmingly high proportion* are somehow less capable of definition than *many* and *nearly all*, or are in some other way inferior subjects for study in the semantics of nonstandard quantification. This is somewhat like treating one set of commonplace expressions as serious candidates for semantic analysis, and classing others as vague or nebulous. Obviously this is undesirable, and underlines the general problem of whether it is possible to treat quantifying statements in a uniform way within a formal framework.

Keenan and Stavi (1986) in their general treatment specifically exclude such commonplaces as *many* and *few* along with other expressions such as *a surprisingly large number of*, and *too many, too few*, and so on. These they term *value judgement determiners*, indicating that they are used to form statements that can only be judged as true or false with respect to some restricted state of affairs, which may include an evaluation of what people might expect normally to be the case. In proposing that *many* and *few* are value judgement determiners, they consider the example:

(15) Many tourists visited the zoo today.

They point out that what it conveys may well be different for different circumstances (e.g. in comparison with what is normal for this time of year; what is normal for a rainy day, etc.). They summarise: "Thus one who asserts (15) indicates that he regards the number of visitors as significant, and he may have almost any random reason for that assessment."[4] We illustrated the potential complexity of the notion of significant number earlier. Keenan and Stavi's suggestion is to make this notion central to the meaning of the terms *many* and *few*.

To summarise: We have not attempted to describe recent logical work in any detail; that was not our purpose. Recent work on quantification has attempted to explain which quantifiers might appear in natural language, and to list their properties. We shall discuss some of these properties later on. We noted that such commonplace expressions as *many, few*, and *nearly all* depend upon what things they are determiners of, which makes it difficult to specify their truth conditions. To make matters worse, the class of value-judgement determiners promises to be very large, and although these expressions do have logically interesting properties (to be discussed later), the fact remains that in order to determine the truth of a statement containing one of them, knowledge about specific situations and even the expectations and interests of the interlocutors have to be brought in.

ISSUES INSPIRED BY PRAGMATICS

Implicature

The use of quantifiers and a whole variety of related expressions has been investigated within the domain of pragmatics as well as semantics. Pragmatics is concerned with the beliefs and assumptions that surround communication, and the fundamental distinction on which it is founded is between sentence (or more strictly, the proposition underlying the sentence) and utterance. The semantic work described earlier is concerned with sentences, and each term in a sentence is assumed to have a meaning, the meaning of the sentence being composed of the subsentential components. An utterance is assumed to be an act of communication, grounded in the belief states of both the speaker/writer and reader/listener, and goes beyond what can logically be inferred from the proposition itself. Thus pragmatics is concerned with what it is that a speaker is trying to communicate, and is based on the idea that interlocutors behave according to a set of implicit conversational rules, which Grice (1975) expressed in his well-known maxims. He introduced the idea of implicatures; inviting inferences about what is being said that are nontruth-functional. As an example using quantifiers, consider the proposition *some artists grow vegetables*. This means that at least one and possibly all artists grow vegetables. If they all grew vegetables, then a person who uttered this proposition would have been telling the truth. The sentence is logically true, regardless of what the speaker knows or believes. But it is easy to see that in normal dialogue, if someone chose to say *some artists*, they would not mean *all*. Within the Gricean framework, we might say that when a speaker uses *some X*, there is an implication that either *all X* is not the case and the speaker knows it, or *all X* may be the case, but the speaker only knows that *some X* is the case. In short, the utterance tells the listener about the state of knowledge of the speaker.

Most pragmatic studies of quantifiers fall within a more general set of questions about scaleable expressions (Horn, 1972; Harnish, 1979; Gazdar, 1979; Kempson, 1975). Just as *some X* implicates *not all X*, so in some contexts, at least, to say you like someone might implicate that you do not love them:

A: Do you love John?
B: I like him.

This general notion has been termed scalar implicature (e.g. Hirschberg, 1985), and has resulted in attempts to specify just what conditions must hold for things to be scaleable. One suggestion is that expressions higher up a scale entail what is entailed by expressions below. So, *all X* entails *some X* entails *only a little bit of X*, and so on (e.g. Gazdar, 1979). On this basis, if I say *only a little bit of X* then I implicate *not some X* and more strongly *not all X*. The burden of the scalar approach, then, is to show that the expressions concerned are scaleable. Indeed, there appear to be many things which are intuitively scaleable (attributes, part–whole relations, temporal sequence, and many others, including perhaps precision—see Hirschberg, 1985). This again fits with the view that quantifiers are used to denote positions on a scale, albeit vaguely, but it is an oversimplification to suppose that this is all there is to the vast variety of quantifying expressions. In general, then, the burden of the pragmatics approach is to go beyond straightforward truth-functional semantics, and investigate implicature and speaker intention.

Quantity and scalar implicature have received considerable attention from workers in pragmatics, and are important for determining when one expression rather than another is chosen when an utterance is produced. However, an inference drawn in order to understand an implicature is neither logically necessary, nor guaranteed to be made by a listener (only the latter is true of a logical statement). Whether the appropriate inferences are drawn is for psychological investigations to confirm. For instance, if *some* implicates *not all*, it could be reasoned that some failures of syllogistic reasoning can be explained in terms of the importation of the implicature into the representation of the premises. While this may happen sometimes, it certainly does not always happen. More generally, the relation between intuitions about pragmatics and the psychological representations of meaning or significance that obtain in interlocutors during dialogue requires careful attention. For example, if, as has been claimed, someone who utters *not many people came to the party* is effectively saying that the proposition that *many people came to the party* is false (denial: a pragmatic phenomenon), then as psychologists we might ask, who thought that many would have come? We shall encounter this issue in Chapter 6.

Pragmatics and Vagueness

An issue for both pragmatics and semantics is vagueness. It has profound influence on the kinds of inferences which people draw. In contrast to ambiguity, where there is more than one possible meaning for an utterance, vagueness occurs when something cannot be understood in at least one precise way. Thus the expression *many* is vague to the extent that it might be acceptable for 70%, 80%, 60%, and so on. In terms of expression-to-scale mappings, everything that we have considered is vague. Closely related to the notion of vagueness is that of precision. Taking as an example the notion of probability, it is clear that to say $P = 0.8$ is more precise than to say "there is a high probability", and this is the dominant way in which vague natural language expressions are thought of as being imprecise. It is noteworthy, however, that precision is a relative thing, and that for some purposes, knowing that $P = 0.8$ might be insufficiently precise, and that $P = 0.82$ (or 0.80) might be considered more suitably precise. What this kind of reasoning leads to is that to call something precise is to say that for some purpose, the quantity expression relies on a sufficiently differentiated scale to be maximally useful. Thus, for example, if one is ridge-walking in the hills, to be told that the distance between two peaks is 3.5 kilometres is sufficiently informative, but to be told that it is 3.502 kilometres is bizarre. In short, what counts as acceptable precision depends on the situation, and it is possible to be overprecise (again violating some version of Grice's maxim of quantity). In fact, a suitable level of precision is necessarily a function of the graininess of the scale of measurement and the applicability of that level of graininess to what is being measured. In the case of ridge-walking, for instance, the reason for 3.502 kilometres being too accurate is that this level of accuracy is too great to correspond to the reality of walking. It is easy to add or subtract 2 metres or more from a route just by going around a boulder! If we believe that the person who specified a tricky bit of ridge as being 57 metres long is speaking in good faith, then we may go on to infer that there is only one way to move along the ridge (which with difficult ridges is often true). Thus, the level of precision an utterance is given may well induce specific patterns of inference.

Indeed, some recent psychological work has been carried out that shows that the precision of an answer has an impact on how a listener might perceive a speaker. When answering questions, a speaker's replies depend on how much the speaker knows (among other things), but they also *show* something about this knowledge. There are few places where this is more obvious than in answers that relate to the precision of quantities. Compare the following ways of answering the question of when Einstein was born:

(16) Einstein was born towards the end of the 19th century.
(17) Einstein was born on 14 March, 1879.

(17) is more exact than (16). Arguably, if one heard (17) as an answer, then one would suppose the speaker to have a level of knowledge more "expert" in some sense than on the basis of (16). This raises an interesting question. Clearly, the time spanned by the precision level in (16) is greater than the time spanned by the precision level of (17), which means that disregarding assumptions about the knowledge level of the speaker, (16) is more likely to be correct than (17). Purely logically, a broad statement must be true if the specific version is true, but may also be true even if the exact formulation is wrong. On the other hand, if a listener assumes that precision correlates with expertise, then the listener may have more faith in the more precise answer. The psychologist Teigen (1990) calls this the "preciseness paradox", and he investigated it empirically. In one study, Teigen set a problem that stated it was possible to divide the 99 members of the Icelandic parliament into "conservative" and "socialistic". He asked people to state which of the following statements they would put most faith into:

Helga: There was a socialistic majority.
Gunhild: There was a nonconservative majority
Vigdis: There was a conservative majority
Heida: The conservatives got between 55 and 60 representatives.

The majority of respondents said that they would put most faith into Heida's description. The reasons offered were to the effect that Heida's description merited most faith because she appears to be the best informed. There is thus a preference for the most exact statement because it signals expertise. Other studies indicate a similar pattern.

Of course, Heida's statement is respected only because there are no reasons to believe that she is anything other than well informed. This is because expert statements are typically true, presented with confidence, and are precise. However, Teigen went on to investigate the possible overlap of this pattern with bluffs and wild guesses, which he claims are *typically* false (untrustworthy), but confidently voiced, and highly specified. This pattern mimics most of the surface characteristics of expert assertion, of course. In a very elegant study, Teigen changed his question from which description merits most faith to which description merits most scepticism. In the Icelandic politics example given earlier, the pattern was exactly the same as with the faith condition. That is, people will assert that they have most faith in the specfic case, and (independently) that they are most sceptical of that case. Thus it would appear that if one is looking for reasons to have faith in a proposition, then specificity suggests expertise, which in turn meets that criterion. In contrast, if one is looking for reasons to be sceptical, then precision may signal suspicion. Teigen's example nicely shows how psychological investigation of some of the ideas produced by an analysis of the pragmatics of communication can reveal important consequences of vagueness and precision. There is obviously more to vagueness than simple inexactness.

An argument similar to this may be made for quantifiers *per se*. There may well be occasions on which it is better to use a vague quantifier rather than an exact number, if the precision level of the number would invite the wrong inferences. Furthermore, expressions that combine numbers and natural language modifiers may be used to signify degrees of precision, for example, expressions such as *about X, roughly X, approximately X*, and so on. These expressions are themselves sometimes called *approximatives*, and have been given an interesting semantic analysis by Wierzbicka (1986).[5] Among other interesting observations Wierzbicka notes that *approximately X* may be taken as implying that accuracy is possible (hence known to the speaker) while *roughly X* does not imply this. Thus the approximative chosen has the potential to convey something about the relevant level of accuracy, or the level of accuracy that the speaker may be presumed to achieve. The implications of this for attributions like those investigated by Teigen have received little or no attention to date.

LOOKING AHEAD

In the following chapters we start with a more thorough examination of work carried out in the tradition that assumes that quantifiers denote quantities. We then shift emphasis to the idea that listeners may not necessarily compute amounts at all, and that speakers may not intend them to do so. The argument is taken up that quantifiers primarily and systematically control the patterns of inference that a listener might develop. This leads us into a mixture of research from psychology, pragmatics, and logic. Our emphasis will be essentially psychological. The basic questions being asked are: How do quantifiers contribute to comprehension? What is the advantage of the great variety of quantifiers? What progress has been made towards specifying when one quantifier will be used rather than another?

NOTES

1. Not only can a quantifier denote different proportions when uttered in exactly the same context and when only one of those proportions is in fact the case, it can also be used to denote an unknown proportion which nevertheless is known to be within a range. That is, quantifiers may be imprecise, but they are also vague. When we say quantifiers are vague or that they vaguely denote proportions, we mean that they can be used to denote a vague proportion in a precise way. For example, I can say that *"many of the children in my class come from broken homes"*, when the exact number is variable (to the extent that the children in my class change as do their circumstances). *Many* is more precise (accurate) as a descriptor than a numerical value *because* it is vague.

2. (13) and (13′) will be equivalent in truth conditional semantics if their truth values are necessarily equivalent. That is, if when (13) is true, it follows that (13′) is true, and vice versa, then these statements mean the same thing. This is not the case for (12) and (12′) in Truth Conditional semantics, for the reasons stated in the text. Note, however, that (13) and (13′) do not necessarily mean the same thing in a psychological account of meaning. Although their truth values may be interdeterminable, the truth of a statement is not the sum total of its meaning. *Some* could denote 20% of quakers and 60% of teetotallers. Each of these satisfies the logical "at least one ..." constraint, but has quite a different meaning in terms of the inferences one might make. If *some* were not a vague quantifier, then truth conditional definitions would be psychologically satisfactory. As we have argued, however, the value of many expressions is tied to the fact that they are vague.

3. Readers who are interested in pursuing this question in a more general framework should see Lakoff's (1987) attack on traditional logical semantics.

4. One is tempted to suppose that the fact that it is raining kangaroos in Edinburgh is a good reason to "regard the number of visitors as significant". The point is that reasons for assessments about the significance of various quantifiers are far from random, unless extralinguistic contextual factors are viewed as a seething mass of unstructured possibilities. Yet, years of psychological research has been dedicated to revealing just how structured such contextual knowledge is.

5. Wierzbicka presents an account of a variety of expressions which she claims can be given clear semantic specifications. She contrasts this with other pragmatic treatments of approximators. It is interesting that a central feature of her treatment is a specification of semantics in terms of what "one might expect", thus introducing expectations into semantics.

CHAPTER TWO

Quantifiers and Quantities

Perhaps the most obvious approach to the meaning of quantifiers, and related expressions such as frequency adverbs, is that they correspond to points on a scale. They may be considered as depicting amounts or proportions, but rather more inexactly than actual numbers might do. In questionnaire research, it is widely recognised that people prefer to answer questions posed with quantifiers or frequency expressions than questions posed with numbers (e.g. Zimmer, 1983). Consequently, there has been a body of work concerned with the mapping of quantifiers onto scales, and much of it is reviewed in this chapter.

Such an approach presupposes the truth of the idea that the meaning of quantifiers is essentially to convey quasi-numerical information. We shall have reason to question this assumption later, but even within the presupposition several questions emerge. How discriminably different are the many quantifying expressions that people use? To what extent do different people give the same values to the same expressions? To what extent are the values that people give to expressions dependent on context?

THE PSYCHOMETRIC APPROACH
Scales and Variability

Because of its obvious application to questionnaire design, there has been steady work attempting to find a set of quantifiers that would optimally discriminate between points on a scale. What quantifiers should be used to provide an interval scale of measurement with a minimal overlap between adjacent items, for instance? A variety of methods has been used in this quest. For instance, Bass et al. (1974) used the psychophysical method of magnitude estimation (e.g. Stevens, 1966), in which subjects were first asked to give a numerical value for the expression *some*, and then to give values for 43 other expressions relative to their value for *some*. Thus, if *some* had been given an (arbitrary) value of 50, and *many* was considered to be twice as many as *some*, then it would be given a value of 100. The rank order of expressions on the scale was the same for various populations of subjects tested, but there was a very large overlap in the numerical values given for the expressions. If a small number of carefully chosen expressions are considered it is possible to produce a discriminable set. But even with as few as nine expressions that optimally discriminated points on the scale, there was a mean overlap of nearly 20% between adjacent points. Thus these early results indicate the difficulties associated with trying to find a reasonably large yet clearly discriminable set of quantifiers. The results are typical of scaling studies of quantifiers, regardless of scaling technique employed (see also Hakel, 1969).

We shall return to the issue of interval scaling shortly; first we shall consider sources of variance and any implications for developing an account of the use of quantifiers. As Pepper (1981) pointed out with respect to frequency adverbs, variance may be due to subjects (either within or between), and to the conditions of measurement, including situational context. Within- and between-subject variance is of great importance from the point of view of communication. Because natural language quantifiers are vague, the scale values assigned to any one may vary from time to time within an individual. If between-subject variation is great, then there should be great potential for misunderstanding in communication.

A number of investigators have found that, within individuals, the rank order of magnitude-denoting expressions seems to be preserved from one test period to another, but that ordering is not constant between individuals. Both Beyth-Marom (1982) and Johnson (1973) found that individuals seemed to be consistent in their assignments of numbers to probability expressions, yet these assignments varied from person to person. Similarly, Budescu and Wallsten (1985) had 32 subjects rank 19 probability and frequency expressions on three separate occasions, and showed that individuals produced stable rank orderings, whereas between individuals the rankings showed considerable variability.

Almost all studies of scaling have used designs in which a subject will make several judgements of several stimuli, and this in itself poses a problem, even for the interpretation of the apparent constancy of scale values within individuals, and this makes even the within-subject constancies suspect. It is well documented that when an individual makes more than one judgement on a scaling task, whether making magnitude estimates or using a fixed scale, the spacing given to items on the scale by subjects is dependent upon the range and distribution of items with respect to the scale in question (see especially Helson, 1964; Parducci, 1968; Poulton, 1968, 1973, 1989). Thus Chase (1969) demonstrated effects of whether the stimuli in a judgement set were predominantly high-frequency or predominantly low-frequency influenced the scale values given to the *same* item (Newstead, 1988, reports a similar finding). Processes of comparison and contrast (see especially Poulton, 1973, 1989, for illustrations) may very well produce rank-order constancies that are spurious from the point of view of meaning and communication. Consider the following hypothetical example. Everyone would agree that *very few* should be less than *few*. Thus, if *few* were judged by some subject as having a value of 10%, he might judge *very few* as 8%. But the same person might have judged *very few* as 10% if he had not already used this value for *few*. The problem gets worse when one considers the widely differing values offered by people in the same linguistic community. In short, within-subject scaling has to be treated with care, as one could obtain reliably different scale positions for a set of expressions within individuals, largely because of the contextual influences of the other items. This would give a spurious impression of how scale meanings might be represented within individuals, and would clearly be meaningless from a between-subject perspective. If individuals judged only one expression in some context, then it may (and does) turn out that many expressions are effectively impossible to discriminate in terms of the scale values they might be taken as denoting (Moxey & Sanford, 1992).

Such considerations of item-context effect on scaling bring us face-to-face with two ways of thinking about the problem of variability between individuals, with two associated research strategies. Budescu and Wallsten (1985, p. 401) suggest that "theoretical issues regarding the use and understanding of probability phrases are more appropriately investigated at the level of individuals than of groups". This might be true for some purposes, for instance to demonstrate individual consistencies in interpretation. However, the other point of view is that language is for communication, and that utterances are produced by speakers for the benefit of listeners. When a speaker uses a particular quantifier or probability term, he may not know precisely how this will be interpreted by the listener, but only have a general idea. So, in normal communication, understanding the possible range of interpretations that the language community might give to an expression is important. For instance, an individual may believe that *very few X* signals fewer X than does *few X*, but variability in the community may be such that a speaker could not assume that there was much to choose between these expressions, in terms of quantity at least. If the vast number of quantifiers, frequency adverbs, and probability expressions give great scope for confusion in terms of scale values, much of their communicative impact may perhaps be found in other aspects of their meaning. This claim is investigated in later chapters.

Membership Functions

A sophisticated progression from scaling studies is the measurement of membership functions. Wallsten and his colleagues (see especially Wallsten, Budescu, Rapoport, Zwick, & Forsyth, 1986a) made use of such functions as a way of describing an individual's representation of probability phrases. The argument is intended to generalise to all scaleable natural language domains. A membership function is essentially a function depicting how well a term maps onto scale values over some entire scale, and it stems from the fuzzy logic developed by Zadeh (1975; McCawley, 1981), in which it is assumed that membership in a category need not be all-or-none, but is graded. Suppose that a particular statement (say *X is probable*) is considered as denoting some value(s) in the probability interval [0,1]. There will be some parts of the range (say $P = 0.3$) that are not acceptable as part of the concept of *probable*. Such values score zero on the membership function. Other values, such as $P = 0.8$, may be definitely in the concept, and these will (by choice) be given the value 1 in the membership function. In other words, the function value ranges from zero for probability values definitely not in the concept to 1 for values that definitely are in the concept. A well-defined concept would have a membership function that only took the values 0 or 1, but with poorly defined (vague, or fuzzy) concepts, intermediate values are possible. Thus, for the term *likely*, for instance, the membership value can be thought of as perhaps being 1 for $P = 0.7$, 0 for $P = 0.4$, but say 0.6 for $P = 0.5$. This is the interpretation Wallsten et al. give to the notion of membership function. Some membership functions for some quantifiers are shown in Fig. 2.1, (and serve to illustrate once again the vast amount of overlap among quantifiers scaled in this way). Wallsten et al. (1986a) used various empirical techniques to estimate membership functions for a variety of expressions.

These investigators hold the view that if membership functions are the same over different tasks (that is, performance on one task can be predicted from performance on another task), then the scale values must represent the meaning of the terms to the subjects. They claim to have shown a variety of constancies, reinforcing this claim. For instance, Wallsten et al. (1986a) used a method in which subjects judged the degree to which one probability rather than another was described by a probability term (e.g.

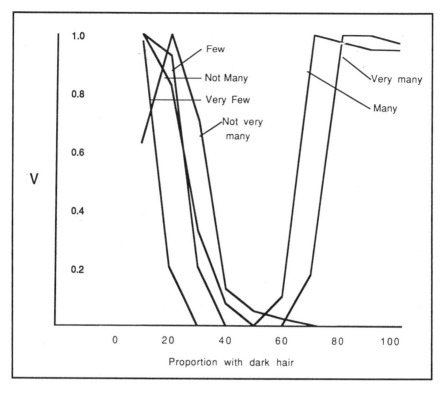

FIG. 2.1. Membership functions for six quantifiers, from one individual. The high degree of overlap in the low-ranking quantifier groups is typical of all subjects. V is the mean value of five estimates of degree of category membership in the range 0–1. (Data from Sanford, Moxey, & Matteson, unpublished.)

how well *doubtful* described a probability of 0.4 or 0.3). In another study, the degree to which one term rather than another described a specific probability was measured (e.g. how well a probability of 0.4 is described by *doubtful* or *probable*). In both cases, a paired-comparison method was used. Comparisons were made between the membership functions derived, and showed a high degree of constancy over individuals, but considerable variability between subjects. In another similar study, Rapoport, Wallsten, and Cox (1987) compared pair comparison with direct membership estimation, in which on a given trial an expression in question was presented along with a probability value, and a direct value elicited by the subject positioning a slider on a scale of *not at all* to *absolutely*. For a given individual, roughly similar functions were obtained for the two tasks, although there was more discrepancy with these tasks than in the Wallsten et al. (1986a) study.

Wallsten and his colleagues believe that the membership functions they obtained represent the meanings of probability expressions for individuals. To the extent that different methods of eliciting the functions produce the same results, it might be supposed that the position is substantiated. However, different methods do not give quite the same results and so the position is weakened. Furthermore, it seems absurd to suppose that the meanings of probability expressions (in truth-conditional terms) can be captured by functions on a 0–1 scale. As Fox (e.g. 1986, 1991) has pointed out, probability terms have established categorical meanings (distinguishing, for instance, *possible* and *probable*) that cannot be captured in the unidimensional framework. The rich semantics underlying these expressions has been obscured by the adoption of the unidimensional assumption, and Fox has argued that treatments of uncertainty in expert systems, for instance, founders if this semantics is ignored. Despite its technical elegance, the approach of Wallsten et al. (1986a) certainly runs into the same problem.

CONTEXT AS A SOURCE OF VARIATION OF MAPPING

Apart from the fact that numerical values that subjects assign to quantifiers depend on the composition of the stimulus set to which they are exposed, a more substantial blow to the idea that a set of quantifiers might produce an equal-interval scale comes from studies of situational context as a source of variance in expression-to-scale-mapping behaviour. Such contextual effects are also of major theoretical significance, of course. In Chapter 1, we presented some intuitive arguments to suggest a dependence of expression-to-scale-mapping on the situation being described. For instance, *many carol singers outside my door* might be of the order of 10–20, whereas *many soldiers killed in battle* would normally be interpreted as hundreds. Empirical data demonstrating this is surprisingly sparse, possibly because as a knock-down argument it is so powerful. We shall begin by examining context effects for frequency and probability expressions, and then for quantifiers of amount *per se*.

Context Effects with Frequency and Probability Terms

Newstead and Collis (1987) examined the dependence of numbers reported in a scaling task on context. One question was about the number of visits someone might make to the cinema in a year, and the other was about the number of visits someone might make to the USA. They found, for instance, that to *visit the cinema often* represents more times per year than to *visit the USA often*, as our intuitive arguments suggested. The advantage of experiment over intuition is that we see just how limited the contextual effect turns out to be. In the Newstead and Collis study the effect was restricted to *often* and *always* with the lower-denoting expressions showing no context effect at all.

These results raise a number of questions. First, consider the possible basis for making a numerical estimate to such enquiries. In order for one to estimate the number of visits per year, given that *one goes to the cinema often*, some baseline is called for, preferably a plausible maximum. A good anchor value for this might be once a week, which would give less than 50 as a typical reply. This is not so feasible for going to America: A person who went once a week and stayed a day would be away more than a quarter of the year and be permanently jet-lagged. In short, expected rates, based on plausible guesses or real information, may provide a standard against which frequency expressions are calibrated. It would be interesting to know how subjects make choices in these cases, to see if or how responses relate to situation-specific knowledge in more detail. The baseline argument opens up the possibility that context effects such as these result from (1) fixing some sort of baseline, and (2) applying the frequency expression to the number associated with that baseline. This is similar to the idea of a manifold introduced by Altham (1971; see Chapter 1). Fortunately, there is experimental data on this, which will be described shortly.

The other interesting detail is that expressions denoting small frequencies (such as *rarely*) in the Newstead and Collis (1987) study did not differentiate from each other, and were not a function of situation. Perhaps numbers for these expressions are produced with reference to lower bounds, which in the present scenarios are both zero. Indeed, the frequencies associated with *never* are zero in both cases. In complete contrast, frequencies for *always* are 50 times for the cinema, and 20 times for visiting the USA, evidence for the kind of asymmetry that we are claiming.

Rather more research has been done in which subjects give *percentage* estimates of frequency and probability rather than numbers, and here too there are context effects. The possibility of context effects with percentages is just as plausible as it was with absolute numbers: Parducci (1968) suggested that a student thinking of contraceptive failure might regard 5% of the time as *often*, whereas 5% of the time missing lectures might be considered *almost never*. In a more systematic study, Pepper and Prytulak (1974; see also Pepper, 1981) asked subjects to give specific numbers from 0 to 100 to define five frequency expressions. The expressions were presented in six contexts, which had different baserates, or norms, associated with them. Low-frequency events included *a sizeable earthquake in California*, moderate frequency events included *a student missing breakfast*, and the highest frequency events were things such as *a shooting in a Hollywood Western*. A condition with "no context" was also included. The results showed a strong relation between baserate estimates and the numerical values given to expressions. For frequency expressions that rank high in terms of the frequency they denote, the higher the baserate, the higher the frequency they were taken as denoting. Effects on lower-ranking expressions were not reliable. This result matches the intuition that *frequently* would be used for a lower frequency when baserate is low (as in, say, contraceptive failure rate) than it would when baserate is high (as in, say, the chances of death in the event of a heart attack).

A further baserate effect was demonstrated by Newstead and Collis (1987), who compared statements about feeling happy versus suicidal, assuming that it is more common to feel happy than to feel suicidal. They used questions like the following:

If I *sometimes* feel happy, I feel happy ... % of the time.

There was a main effect of emotion type on the proportions taken as the meanings of the adverbs, with *happy* producing higher proportions in response to the same expressions than *suicidal*. Interestingly, *never* produced 13% in the happy context, whereas for the suicidal context it produced 0%. *Always* produced 92% in the happy context, but produced 85% in the suicidal context. Taken at face value, a generalisation such as *I'm always happy* seems to mean 92% of the time, but to say *I'm never happy* means I'm happy 13% of the time: One needs to be happy more often than one has to be suicidal to allow either generalisation. There was no tendency for the context effect to be restricted to expressions denoting higher frequencies, unlike all comparable studies. There is no explanation for this discrepancy at present.

An extensive replication of the baserate effects observed by Pepper and Prytulak (1974) was reported by Wallsten, Fillenbaum, and Cox (1986b), both for frequency expressions and for probability terms such as *probable* and *possible*. They devised scenarios in which events could take on two levels of probability, as in:

What is the probability of snow in Montreal in (one of the following) October/December?

The authors obtained independent probability estimates for these types of contrasts in a large number of situations, and then tested estimates of likelihood corresponding to natural language expressions such as:

Snow is likely to fall in Montreal in October (probability expression).
and
Snow frequently falls in Montreal in October (frequency expression).

In the face of such statements, subjects had to manipulate a slider on a line to express what they thought "the expert who produced the statement had in mind" within the range 0–1. The results showed an effect of baserate on probability judgement (pointer position) for a given expression, provided that the expression was one that seems to denote a higher proportion of probability. If baserate was low, then estimates were lowered. Wallsten et al. (1986b) carried out some straightforward model-fitting, and claimed that the interpretations "appeared to represent some kind of average of the meaning of the expression and the base rate" (p. 571). Wallsten et al.'s statement expresses a commitment to the view that the adverbs and probability terms have a basic scale meaning, and that this is somehow distorted by baserate.

Given that there is good evidence for normative baserate effects for frequency and probability terms, it would be expected that individual's idiosyncratic baserates could have comparable effects. Were this so, individual variation in baserate could go some way towards explaining individual variation in interpretation. Goocher (1965; 1969) demonstrated that subjects who do not like an activity, or do not participate in it, will use higher-denoting expressions to describe the same frequency of activity as subjects who do like the activity, or participate in it. This may be due to a tendency to perceive one's own frequency in an activity as the average, or norm. Thus, if a subject does not like dancing, he may think that dancing on 10% of possible occasions is more than normal, and will describe this amount using a frequency adverb that indicates this fact (such as *often*). A dancing buff would not make the same judgement. These data are consistent with a view that norms determine expression-to-number-mappings, and extend the argument that some norms, at least, might well be based on the individuals' own experience (and perhaps the experience of their immediate reference subculture).

Quantifiers and Context

As with frequency adverbs, the simplest view of meanings of quantifiers is that they denote proportions or numbers (albeit fuzzily). Empirical investigations have been carried out using both types of response format and both show context dependency. In Chapter 1 (p. 11) we saw that formulations of *many* and *nearly all* in terms of number presented difficulties. As Altham (1971) noted, and as was evident in our anecdotal discussion, if a quantifier is taken as denoting a number or range of numbers, then the value(s) denoted will be a function of the situation described, and possibly of the set size.

There is empirical work on both of these issues. Hörmann (1983) invited subjects to say how many things were denoted by the quantifiers *einige*, *mehrere*, and *ein paar* (*some*, *several*, and *a few*). The results showed the numbers reported for a given quantifier to be a function of the size of the objects and of the spatial situations surrounding the objects. For instance, with the expression *a few*, subjects gave higher numerical values for the situations furthest down this list:

A few people standing before the hut.
... before the house.
... before the city hall.
... before the building.

Hörmann believed that the effect was due to the relative sizes of people and what they stood in front of. Therefore, if elephants are substituted for people, then the value of *a few* is correspondingly reduced. He also noted that mean values for *a few grains of sand* and *a few people*, for instance, could be similarly ordered. While it is tempting to suppose that the numbers that people produce in these tasks are at least partially a result of the relative physical size of objects, it is possible that all of Hörmann's results can be explained in terms of the expectations of his subjects, which may only be incidentally correlated with size. Indeed, Clark (1991) has suggested that "when we hear *several crumbs* or *several mountains* we imagine a scene typical of crumbs or mountains". The response one gives to *several* will clearly depend on the situation imagined—on what one would expect.

Subjects should expect that a group of people standing in front of a city hall will be larger than a group standing in front of a hut because in the past groups of people in front of halls were likely to have been larger than those in front of huts. Likewise, subjects will expect a few grains of sand to be a larger number than a few people because situations involving grains of sand (e.g. a handful of sand) normally imply more grains than the number of people implied in situations involving people (such as people sitting in a classroom). Of course, the physical size of a hut versus a town hall, or a person versus a grain of sand, may contribute to some extent towards our expectations about those situations. For example, we may have experienced larger groups of people in front of a hall because it is not possible for very large numbers of people to be standing in front of a hut. Nevertheless, it is perhaps the expectation itself that influences one's interpretation of the quantifier. To test this notion compare the following:

(1) Some people standing in front of the fire station.
(2) Some people standing in front of the cinema.

Although the frontage of the average fire station is likely to be about as large as the average cinema, it is quite likely that we expect more people to be standing in front of the cinema. We would therefore predict that *some* in (2) will denote a larger number than it does in (1).

In a recent study Moxey, Tuffield, and Temple (unpublished) presented independent groups of subjects with sentences similar to (1) and (2), replacing the quantifier *some* with *a few* or *many* for some groups. Four buildings were used in the sentences: (a) fire station, (b) cinema, (c) hairdresser, (d) fish and chip shop. These buildings were chosen on the basis of a pilot study that showed that whereas (a) and (b) are both judged to have large frontages (on a 6-point scale from very small to very large), (c) and (d) are judged to have small ones. In addition, (a)–(d) vary with respect to the number of people subjects expect to be standing in front of them; the estimates of the number of people that might be expected to be standing in front of a fish and chip shop is higher than the number that would be expected in front of a fire station, although the second has a larger frontage. Table 2.1 shows the median and mean estimates given by subjects in the various conditions. These results suggest that it is not size alone, but also expectation that influences estimates. Specifically, the number of people *expected* in front of a large building does influence estimates for *many* and *some*: the more expected, the higher the values given. This does not hold for *a few*. Secondly, the *size* of the building has no (reliable) influence on estimates of *a few*; size does influence the values given to *some* and *many*, but only when a large number of people is expected to be standing in the location in question. Overall, the results seem to suggest that when there is reason to expect a large number of people, or when the maximum number of people can be large (given the size of the building),

TABLE 2.1
Median and Mean Estimates Given by Subjects in the
Moxey, Tuffield, and Temple Study

	Small		Large	
	Low Expectation	High Expectation	Low Expectation	High Expectation
Few	4.0 (5.10)	5.0 (5.30)	5.0 (11.10)	5.0 (5.76)
Some	3.0 (4.25)	4.0 (5.00)	5.0 (6.35)	10.0 (33.60)
Many	10.5 (18.50)	10.5 (13.90)	20.0 (25.40)	51.5 (89.60)

First number is the median; the mean follows in brackets.

then quantifiers denoting higher amounts will produce higher numerical interpretations than they would otherwise. However, the difference between the small building/high expectation and the large building/low expectation is not significant, so size is only a factor when the number of people expected (for whatever reason) is high, as physical size will determine the upper boundary for what it is reasonable to imagine or expect. Thus size is a boundary condition on expectation, but it may or may not correlate with mean expectation, and is not the primary determinant of the numbers produced in this type of experiment.

If objects and situations clearly influence the numbers assigned to quantifiers, and if the quantifiers do not denote a fixed number (or range of numbers), do they then denote fixed proportions or ranges of proportions? Certainly, an increase in absolute number with increased set size could be the result of a fixed proportion underlying a quantifier. This is compatible with Hörmann's (1983) results, for instance, and with Altham's analysis (p. 11). Data bearing on the issue comes from set-size studies, in which people are asked questions such as "how many out of 100 is some?", "how many out of 10,000?", and so on. Newstead, Pollard, and Reizbos (1987) carried out such a study using set sizes ranging from 10 to 1000 and a variety of quantifiers. Whereas the numbers that people put to all quantifiers went up with set size, a fixed proportion was not maintained. Rather, the proportions obtained for quantifiers denoting small proportions yielded relatively smaller proportions for larger set sizes. Proportion was maintained for quantifiers denoting larger proportions, however. These results appear to show that the proportions associated with the expressions are not fixed, but depend on response set size. As Newstead et al. (1987) point out, from an applications point of view the results cast yet more doubt on the possibility of developing an interval scale using natural language quantifiers. They offer no theory of the effects, however. Granularity of the scale might have an effect with very small response sets. Consider a set size of 10, for instance. If *a few of the beads* means about 15% of the beads, then this translates into 1.5 beads. Rounding up to 2 beads would give a value of 20%. Such reasoning could explain Newstead et al.'s results, but only for very small set sizes. It could not explain larger set-size effects, nor the lack of a set-size effect with the higher-ranking quantifiers. A possible explanation may be based upon a low-ranking quantifier denoting something like a fixed but fuzzy low proportion, but with an upper limit on the absolute number it might denote. Thus, *a few* might mean 15%, but not if that yields an absolute number of 1500, as it would with a set size of 10,000.

Earlier studies of set-size effects on translations into proportions produce similar results for quantifiers indicating small amounts, but also show that quantifiers indicating large amounts seem to denote smaller proportions with increasing set size. Cohen, Dearnley, and Hansel (1958) carried out a study in which they investigated *a lot of*, *some of*, and *a few of*. However, they used child subjects and the overall set sizes were only varied within the range 50 to 200. At the very least, the studies examined here show that quantifiers appear not to denote fixed numbers of things nor fixed proportions of things, although the results of Newstead et al. (1987) do not rule out the possibility that higher-ranking quantifiers may denote fixed proportions.

Any variability in the proportions assigned to expressions as a function of context in a task where subjects have to provide percentage judgements would constitute direct evidence against the view that quantifiers denote fixed percentages (with vagueness introduced through variance). Recent studies carried out on the influence of baseline expectation, using a response format in which subjects give a percentage interpretation, show that higher-ranking quantifiers do indeed show variability in response due to context. Thus Moxey (1986; Moxey & Sanford, 1993) carried out a study in which three levels of expectation were used. The study is unique in that the design was entirely independent-groups. That is, any given subject made only one judgement. This, while expensive in terms of subject numbers, has the advantage of removing the production of fine-grained scales as a result of within-subject contrast effects. The three situations used were *the proportion of people who might enjoy a party, the proportion of an audience that might be swayed by a political speech*, and *the proportion of female doctors in a local hospital*. Three independent groups of subjects provided baseline estimates of these percentages. This was done by presenting the information in vignettes that subjects imagined to be snippets from news reports, as shown below:

"The residents association's Xmas party was held last night in the town hall."
Question: What percentage of the residents do you think enjoyed the party?

"At yesterday's party conference, Mr. Cameron spoke about the effects of education cuts on British universities."
Question: What percentage of the audience do you think were influenced by Mr. Cameron's speech?

"A survey has recently been carried out to find out whether or not female students prefer to be examined by female doctors."
Question: What percentage of the local doctors do you think are female?

The estimates given were reliably different for the three contexts and we can therefore ague that people have reliably different expectations about the proportions. The average estimate for the guests was 66%; for the audience 50%; and for the female doctors 27%. In the main study, subjects were presented with the same snippets of text except that a quantified statement was added:

> [Quantifier] of those who attended the party enjoyed what might be called the social event of the year.
> [Quantifier] of his audience were convinced by his conclusions.
> [Quantifier] of the local doctors are female

[Quantifier] was replaced in each of these statements by one of the following: *few, a few, very few, only a few, quite a few, not many, many, very many, a lot*, and *quite a lot*. Fifteen subjects were assigned to each of the resulting 30 conditions.

As Fig. 2.2 shows, the quantifier presented to subjects had a significant overall effect on the proportion reported.

The difference is restricted to high-denoting quantifiers; there was no remotely reliable difference between the values given to *very few, a few, few, not many*, and *only a few*. We emphasise that this means there is no difference between *very few* and *few* for two independent groups of 45 subjects, for example! Note that even if variability is introduced as an explanation, this is a little like admitting that when an individual says *very few X*, he or she might just as well say *few X*, given that a listener would have no way of discriminating the two (or *a few*, or *not many*, come to that). If we wish to support the plausible hypothesis that these different expressions mean different things, there is little point in looking for the difference in terms of expressed percentages. It is worth reiterating that this problem is not an artefact of using independent groups, although between-subject variance may be expected to be greater than within-subject variance. Rather, it is the fine-grain scaling results obtainable by within-subject measures that might be more properly thought of as artefactual. Thus, a belief that *very few X* is fewer than *few X* (numerically) is not much use if it is not revealed in a reasonable sample of the language community.

An effect of context is also revealed in Fig. 2.2. The interaction of context with quantifier is due almost entirely to the low baserate condition, and is restricted to the five quantifiers denoting larger amounts. Thus, *many, very many, a lot, quite a few*, and *quite a lot* are all reported as denoting smaller percentages in the context where subjects' expectations were low. These results are broadly consistent with those found with probability expressions and frequency adverbs (Pepper & Prytulak, 1974; Wallsten et al., 1986b). Low baserate expectations result in lower percentage translations by subjects, but these are detectable only for those expressions that are associated with high frequencies, probabilities, and proportions.

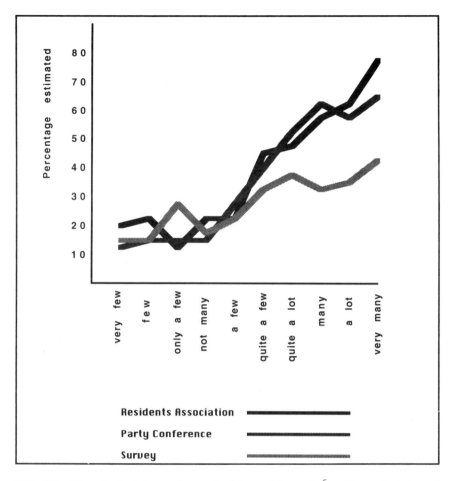

FIG. 2.2. The effect of baserate on the interpretation of quantifiers. Ordering of quantifiers is post-hoc, from least mean value (lowest ranking) to greatest mean value. Each point comes from an independent group. (Adapted from Moxey & Sanford, 1993, with permission.)

A similar study was carried out by Moxey, Sanford, and Grant (in prep.), this time using 10 different scenarios and the 10 quantifiers described earlier (100 data points). A given subject contributed to 10 data points by receiving a particular quantifier and a particular scenario only once (thus allowing an individual 10 combinations). Although not completely independent-groups, this study does allow a further test of the influence of context on the values put to quantifiers. There was a strong relationship between baseline and the interpretation given to the quantifiers: the higher the baseline, the higher the value given to the quantifier. Once again, the effects were greatest on the higher-ranking quantifiers. Straight lines were fitted to the 10 data points for each quantifier, and the linear correlation and the slopes of these lines, shown in Fig. 2.3, provide a summary of this aspect of the study. There does appear to be a weak relationship to context, even for low-ranking quantifiers.

To conclude, several studies show contextual effects on quantifier interpretation. As was the case for frequency adverbs and probability expressions, whether the response format is to produce absolute numbers of percentage judgements, baserate correlates positively with value given, especially in quantifiers that tend to denote higher proportions or numbers in a situation. Such results show that numerical interpretations given to quantifiers do not make up an interval scale; they can be rank-ordered up

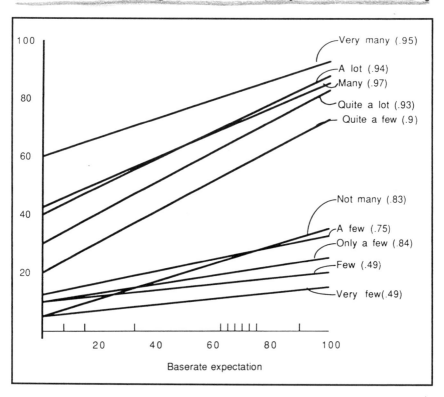

FIG. 2.3. Best straight line fits for estimates of 10 quantifiers over 10 baserates. Bracketed numbers are correlations, all of which are statistically reliable apart from those for Few and Very few. The points are omitted for clarity; the diagram is designed to show that all quantifiers show at least some dependence on context, although it is clear that the lower-ranking expressions show a much weaker dependence in terms of slope. (Data from Moxey, Sanford, & Grant, unpublished.)

to a point, but there is a great deal of overlap, even with the small sets investigated here.

Context Effects with Generalisations

Questions of context effects also arise with generalisations, in which the quantification is implicit:

(3) Ukrainians are tired of Russian domination.
(4) Americans like to eat hamburgers.

It is obvious that these statements may be considered acceptable in normal use without the predicates being true of all Ukrainians and all Americans. However, if such statements are not to be taken as universal, the question arises whether there is anything systematic that can be said about what the truth conditions for such generalisations might be. Abelson and Kanouse (1966; see also Kanouse, 1972) report an investigation of this question. Consider the following:

(5) Students have parties.

Most people would probably think this is a fair generalisation, but would not want to accept it as a universal. They might rather believe that *most students have occasional parties,* for instance. Using statements with a variety of subjects and objects bound by a variety of verbs, Abelson and Kanouse had subjects check off the quantifiers in the following frame to establish what would be the acceptable minimum for the generalisations to be true:

All	Xs	verb	most	Ys
Most	Xs	verb	most	Ys
Many	Xs	verb	many	Ys
Some	Xs	verb	some	Ys
A few	Xs	verb	a few	Ys
One or two	Xs	verb	one or two	Ys

One of the materials presented might mean replacing Xs verb Ys with *artists avoid magazines,* for example. Abelson and Kanouse do not give a specific value for this instance, but readers are invited to try it. To us, it seems that *some artists avoid most magazines* is a plausible minimum! Suppose now that we replace *artists avoid magazines* with *artists like magazines,* and invite subjects to perform the same task. According to Abelson and Kanouse's results we should now find that *most artists like some magazines* is more acceptable than *some artists like most magazines*. As the above example suggests, one source of variance in this study was the verb. Abelson and Kanouse also varied the subject and object of the verb to yield statements such as *mothers like choral music*. However, these subject/object manipulations did not lead to significant differences in the quantifiers chosen by subjects.

Abelson and Kanouse's main argument concerns the effect of a verb, such as *avoid* or *like*, on the acceptability of generalisations concerning that verb.[1] The quantifier study was designed to discover the level of evidence required of the subject and object of the verb, in order for the statement to be deemed acceptable by readers. It was found that the quantifiers selected by subjects, like the acceptability of generalised (implicitly quantified) statements, varied with the type of verb used (see Abelson & Kanouse, 1966, for further details). For our present purpose, the most important finding reported in this study is that the verb contained in a statement influences one's interpretation of quantifiers implicit in the statement. Although the verb is a limited aspect of the (linguistic) context, Abelson and Kanouse's work also suggests that other contextual factors may also play a role, e.g. whether or not the implicitly quantified statement forms part of an inductive or a deductive argument.

The verbs themselves are not the only source of variance, and it is arguable that an analysis in terms of the significance of the utterance for inference in general may play a role in how it is assessed. For example, for many people in the West, a statement such as the following may be considered true if any Arab country had nuclear weapons:

(7) Arab countries have nuclear weapons.

In contrast, the following is more likely to be considered by many as true only if it holds for the majority of Western countries:

(8) Western countries have nuclear weapons.

The argument is that the variety of Arab countries may not be very well differentiated by many Westerners, so, in a sense, one instance stands for all. In contrast, the differentiation of Western countries is likely to be much better appreciated in the West. Obviously, generalisation goes hand-in-hand with the differentiation of the entities over which the generalisation is meant to hold. On these grounds, we might expect the opposite results for judgements made in the Arab world.

Context can also influence the interpretation of the implicit quantification of frequency. For someone to be truthfully called a murderer, for instance, requires only one act of murder, but for someone to be called generous requires generosity on many possible occasions. In a study of the implicit quantification of personality traits, Gidron, Koehler, and Tversky (1991) showed that in general undesirable trait statements were deemed to require the behaviour less frequently than desirable trait statements in order to be considered true. This is consistent with undesirable character traits being deviations from the norm, so it is socially useful to label the deviant behaviour even when it occurs with low frequency. A full account of trait-classification phenomena remains to be established (see also Rothbart & Park, 1986).

CONCLUDING REMARKS

There is ample evidence that the numerical interpretations given to quantifiers are situation-specific. Within what we have termed the psychometric tradition, the values elicited from people have been thought of as key aspects of meaning. Early in the history of the approach, Mozier (1941; also Jones & Thurstone, 1955) suggested that context was noise, and that if values were found for the same expression in many different contexts, then the mean of the distribution would represent the true meaning of that quantifier. Others have voiced the view that quantity terms have true numerical meanings, and that when an utterance containing them is encountered, the interpretation is a function of the basic meaning and the prior probability given by the context (for instance, Zimmer, 1983). Wallsten et al. (1986b) appear to hold similar views, seeing interpretation as some sort of weighted average of context-free true meaning and prior expectation. The detail of what they propose is somewhat difficult to discern, however.[2]

Our view is that the empirical separation of context-dependent numerical interpretation and core meaning is not possible. As Clark (1991) points out, we have no direct access to word meaning as there is no such thing as "no context" for a linguistic expression. Researchers who ask subjects the meaning of an expression in a seemingly "empty context", e.g. *How many is many?*, are really dealing with the unknown context rather than no context. In fact, this is consistent with a pilot study carried out in our lab in which subjects were asked to indicate percentages for quantifiers and then were asked to indicate on a separate sheet whether or not they imagined a set in completing the task. More than half of our subjects reported imagining a set of 100 people (no doubt because they were asked to give a percentage (1–100) and because the task was set in a lecture hall where large sets of people are easily imagined).

Another facet of the psychometric approach is the search for a function that relates core numerical meaning to numerical interpretation:

$$Q \text{ (interpreted)} = f \left[Q(\text{core}), \text{baserate} \right]$$

Although there is a rough positive relation between baserate and interpretation, we believe that the search for a mathematical formulation may not be of much value. Essentially, our view is that core meaning may best be understood in terms of truth conditions that only utilise quantity information in a relatively crude way, and that more precise numerical translations, such as required by the psychometric approach, is a response to only one kind of interpretation, which is perhaps not the most typical.[3] Of course, this claim does not mean that the use of numerical information is without its uses. Indeed, in some interactions, proportions and numbers may be important. Furthermore, quantifiers obviously convey some quantitative information, and this will surely be reflected to some extent in the numbers produced in the judgement tasks. It is just that we doubt whether there is normally an automatic translation of a quantifier into a high-resolution scale value, and thus we believe that the search for a translation function incorporating baserate must be similarly restricted to low resolution.

NOTES

1. Abelson and Kanouse (1966) would argue, for example, that arguments involving the verb *avoid* (which they call a "negative subjective state" verb) will be more effective if a deductive argument is used, rather than an inductive one. Thus we are more likely to conclude that *artists avoid magazines* after (a) than (b):
    (a) All artists are innovative, moody, and forgetful.
       Innovative people avoid magazines.
       Moody people avoid magazines.
       Forgetful people avoid magazines.
    (b) There are three types of artist: commercial, modern, and classical.
       Commercial artists avoid magazines.
       Modern artists avoid magazines.
       Classical artists avoid magazines.
2. These two quotes given an impression of Wallsten's analysis. The claim concerns probability phrases, not quantifiers *per se*:
    "... a probability phrase has a relatively fixed, but vague core meaning for an individual, perhaps such as can be represented by a membership function over the [0,1] interval. This meaning may vary with semantic content."
    This first quote implies that meaning does indeed change with context. However, the article goes on:
    "... in addition, the individual has a vague judgement of the probability

of the event in question, which might also be represented as a function over the [0,1] interval. Upon receiving a verbal probabilistic prediction about the event, the person interprets that prediction as a weighted average of two vague probabilities, that which he or she associates with the expression, and that which he or she associates with the event." (Wallsten et al., 1986b).

3. Weber and Hilton (1990) provide some further evidence that a higher baserate leads to higher interpretations of probability expressions. However, they also found (using illness scenarios) that the more severe the illness being talked about, the higher were the interpretations given to probability expressions. Although the mechanisms for this are poorly understood, Weber and Hilton's data cast additional doubt on the idea that some combination of baserate and basic expression meaning will specify the numerical values that people assign to such expressions in use.

CHAPTER THREE

Scales and Negatives

REMARKS ON SCALING STUDIES

The main purpose of the preceding chapter was to review data collected about the way in which quantifiers can be mapped onto numerical scales, either indicating numbers or percentages. It is apparent that the values that people produce are very variable, so that the task of finding even a small number of quantifiers that produce low numerical overlap is a difficult one. The problem is amplified in that most studies have had subjects make more than one judgement in the scaling tasks. When independent groups are used, so that contrasts cannot be used in the assignment of numbers, even items that on other grounds seem orderable (such as *few* and *very few*; see the section Negativity) are found not to be distinguishable from one another. Intuitively we might expect other expressions to be similarly difficult to differentiate, such as *nearly all* and *not quite all*. In the middle range, *quite a lot* and *quite a few* yielded similar scale values. (In the Moxey and Sanford (1992) study they were not significantly different, and in an unpublished partial replication, McDonald (1990) found no difference between these expressions; any differences found are probably unreliable and due to within-subjects contrast effects.) This all suggests that a mental lexicon in which each quantifier is associated with a distribution of possible numbers, or proportions, would not be a very good explanation of the way in which quantifiers are used, or of how we might characterise their semantics. The same problem holds for any kind of internal analogue representation of a high-resolution (small-grain) scale in which specific quantifiers are associated with specific values or tight distributions of values.

We are not suggesting that a crude ordering of some sort is impossible. On the contrary, it is necessary, and we suggest that people certainly distinguish between high and low amounts (and perhaps some in between) in the face of a statement. But resolution is generally very low, perhaps being generally restricted to high versus low. Furthermore, it is easily argued that in many situations, no fine-grained computation of amount need take place, yet meaningful gradations can be made between assertions using quantifiers. For instance:

A: A lot of people went to the office party last night.
The reply:
B: A lot?

At this point, A remembers that B had hosted a series of extremely successful parties in previous years, which attracted record numbers of people. Remembering this fact, A may modify his utterance to:

A: Well, quite a lot.

This hypothetical interaction appears to show how the interpretation given to *a lot*, picking out a large number, is indeed a value judgement. The recognised mismatch of the frameworks of interpretation of A and B leads A to hedge using "Well … quite …". In a real dialogue, this manoeuvre would probably be recognised by both for what it is: negotiating a claim about the success of a party. Now we do not need to suppose that *a lot* is taken to be interpreted as anything more than something like "*a large number, as large as would normally be expected at a really busy party and maybe more*". Without ever computing such a number (which would be a very irritating thing for B to have done!), the modifier *quite* is readily seen as a scale-down of the strength of the claim. Perhaps *quite a lot* is interpreted as something like "*imagine a lot* (as depicted above); *well, the number there was less than that but not much less*". Whatever the details of the process, it should be clear that quantifiers could convey information relative to some situation that interlocutors have in mind without necessitating the retrieval of fine-grained scale information about number or percentages. Indeed, in Chapter 2 we found that the difference between *few* and *very few* was not reliable, yet it would be universally agreed that on linguistic criteria, *very few* clearly denotes fewer than *few*. The point is, we do not have to know the numeric value of *few* to recognise and use this fact.

The earlier example has the attractive feature of showing how it might be possible to get around the problem of associating scale values with all expressions, or even well-defined values with any quantifiers (except perhaps *all* and *none!*). But the problem is that world-knowledge is made to play a role. In our example, it is the number that would be associated with a busy, successful party. World-knowledge is just that: situation-specific information that embodies norms and expectations about those situations. It is certainly the case that situations and states have normative quantitative values associated with them. For instance:

Children liking Santa: default, all should, as Santa is for children's pleasure.

Number of female surgeons: default, some small proportion, because of beliefs about hiring policies, sex discrimination, etc. Desired value is 50% default.

Children liking ice-cream: default, all should; it is a stereotype.

Even if quantifiers conveyed information restricted to large amount or small amount, the implication for the defaults in the earlier examples is apparent. Either they nearly fit expectation, or they violate it. We believe this to be the basis for the context effects described earlier. But more than this, we suggest that when a quantified statement is understood by people, it is understood in terms of the inferences that it produces with respect to background knowledge, and not in terms of numerical values at all. Numerical values are (usually) only produced when the task demands it. This may seem a little strange as it is obvious that in a comparison task, *few* can be scaled with respect to *very few*. Our view is that the scaling is really one of strength of claim, and not numerical value. Imagine a situation in which the following is said:

(1) John: Is it right that few people came to your graduation?
(2) Fred: Very few.

What John is querying is the idea that a small number of people went to Fred's graduation, and that this is noteworthy, as the ideal attendance is more people. The inference is then that this is a bad state of affairs. John does not know how many people attended. But Fred's reply is to the effect that whatever inferences are being drawn on the basis of a small number, those inferences may be even more important or otherwise more worthy of consideration. The strength of Fred's assertion is greater than John's.

Certainly this type of argument goes some way to providing an alternative to the scale-mapping notion by replacing the idea of a fine-grained quantifier-to-numeric value dictionary with a crude one, and making inference and strength of claim do all of the work. Obviously the view requires much clarification. Specifically, it raises the question of how quantifiers actually control the inferences drawn by listeners (if indeed they do). Much of the remainder of this book is concerned with finding empirical evidence for the control of inferences, our general claim being the rather obvious one that if quantifiers are not very distinguishable from a numerical perspective, because there are so many of them they must be distinguishable on other grounds. We begin our explorations with an examination of linguistic work on quantifier ordering, and on negation. We then describe some psychological studies showing performance correlates of this work.

SCALES BASED ON LINGUISTIC JUDGEMENT

Scales and Implicatures

It has been common in pragmatics to posit orderings such as <*all, most, many, some*> on the basis of the assumption that a statement higher in the ordering (stronger on the scale) entails that lower (weaker) items are true (Gazdar, 1979; Horn, 1972, 1984; Levinson, 1983; see Hirschberg, 1985, for limitations of this approach). Thus, if *all students attend*, then this entails that *some students attend*.[1] In contrast, if *some students attend*, then *all students attend* is not entailed. However, there is an implicature that *not all students attended*. Thus, a statement using an expression lower in the ordering would carry the implicature that anything higher was false. To the extent that tests of entailment and implicature hold in this way over a set of items, we must assume that they form at least an ordinal scale. Using implicatures, the acceptability of the following sentences (for instance) may be considered a test of orderability:

(3) Some, but not many of them attended. (Some < many)
(4) Most, but not all of them attended. (Most < all)
(5) A few, but not a lot of them attended (a few < a lot).

Here, we have made explicit the assumption that the left-hand quantifier has to denote a smaller number or proportion than the right-hand one. Such tests would appear to show that the quantifiers can be discriminated in terms of the size of the set they denote, and to the extent that the orderings are transitive, one might assume that the items form a scale.

With tests like this, there are pairings that seem to be difficult to judge. For instance:

(6) Many, but not a lot of the children, enjoyed the party.
(7) Quite a few, but not quite a lot of the children, enjoyed the party.

These cases are difficult compared with (3), (4), and (5), suggesting that they are not easily separated. Even more interesting are the following:

(8) Many, but not most of the children, enjoyed the party.
(9) Most, but not many of the children, enjoyed the party.

Many readers will find (8) difficult, but they might find it more acceptable than (9). So, one might conclude that if anything, the ordering is many < most (a typical claim). What these examples do show, however, is how complex interpretations might become. For instance, (8) might be acceptable in so far as, relative to some criterion, there were many children who enjoyed the party. But the number of children at the party was so great that the many who did enjoy it were less than half (that is, less than the technical definition of most). If this were true, then (10′) should not be acceptable as the number of children is small:

(10) There were 20 children at a party.
(10′) Many, but not most of the children, enjoyed the party.

With (9), the statement might appear unacceptable, but it would be quite acceptable if the number of children at the party was only 12.[2] In that case, it would seem curious to call 6 *many* in the present context. This example relies on variability of critical set size. However, other more general situational factors may influence the difference between *many* and *most*, and perhaps also their ordering. For instance, it is debatable that *most students are poor* would entail that *more than many students are poor*, i.e. *most* and *many* are hard to separate. In contrast, to say of a culture that *many parents beat their children* certainly does not seem to necessitate that most do. This clearly has to do with a logically necessary property of *most*, meaning more than half, while *many* is free to range to values below at least half. With reason, we might say that *many* may range freely to values below half, being truly a value-judgement expression, yet *most* is not free to fall below this value, which is necessarily its lower limit. What we are suggesting is that these seemingly straightforward procedures for ordering quantifiers rely on judgements that utilise aspects of meaning outside unidimensional scales, and so may not form a very satisfactory basis for drawing conclusions about rank position.

The *but not* construction used earlier follows the implicatures. Some constructions, called *suspenders of implicature* (Horn, 1984), suspend or block the conversational implicatures that might be derived from a statement. For example, *if not* constructions can serve this function:

(11) Some of the staff were there, if not all.
(12) Many of the staff were there, if not all.
(13) A few of the staff were there, if not all.[3]

Such suspenders show that if *some* implies *not all*, then it is indeed an implicature and not an entailment because it is defeasible. On a unidimensional scale account, all smaller proportions might be thought of as implicating not more than that amount (hence not all). So, the suspender can also be used to define scales:

(14) Some of the staff were there, if not most. etc.

The expression *if not all* can be applied to a large number of quantifiers, including *a few, some, quite a lot, quite a few, many, very many, most*, and *nearly all*, as would be expected. However, there is a group of quantifiers with which this expression does not combine. The following are illustrations:

(15) Few of the staff were there, if not all.[*]
(16) Not many of the staff were there, if not all.[*]
(17) Hardly any of the staff were there, if not all.[*]
([*] indicates that the sentence is unacceptable.)

So, it is unreasonable to suppose that *few, not many*, and *hardly any* implicate *not all*. Thus it is not adequate to say that a *small set of A* implicates *not a larger set of A*.

These expressions do combine with *if not none* (or, synonymously, with *if any*), however:

(18) Few of the staff were there, if any/not none.
(19) Not many of the staff were there, if any/not none.

Finally, those that combine with *if not all* do not combine with *if any*; for instance:

(20) A few of the staff were there, if any.[*]

Negativity

This second group of expressions implicates not-none. Because of this, these expressions must admit to the possible interpretation that *none is the case*. These items, which combine with *if any*, have a negative component. Negativity is of course most obvious in the case of terms with explicitly negative affixes, such as *not many*, but also occurs implicitly in *few*. Several different tests that split quantifiers into negative and positive were proposed in a seminal work by Klima (1964). One such test uses a tag question following a simple declarative sentence. Consider the following pair:

(21) Many people went to the meeting, didn't they?
(22) Many people went to the meeting, did they?[*]

(22) is plainly ungrammatical. Compare these cases with:

(23) Not many people went to the meeting, didn't they?[*]
(24) Not many people went to the meeting, did they?

Many is thus considered positive on this test, and *not many* negative. The same test may be applied to all quantifiers.

Another test of negativity is combination with so-called negative polarity items. The argument is a little circular, in that negative polarity items are those expressions that combine with negative statements in simple declarative sentences. However, circularity is partly avoided by the fact that we can use explicit (and hence obvious) negative items to illustrate:

(25) Not many people believe in monetarism anymore.
(26) Many people believe in monetarism anymore.[*]

Here, *not many* is negative, and combines with the polarity item *anymore*. In contrast, *many* is not and does not.[4] In general there is a good correspondence between items classed as negative on this and other tests. Some quantifiers that are positive and negative by these tests are:

Positive: A few, some, quite a few, quite a lot, more than half, many, very many, most, nearly all, all.
Negative: Very few, few, hardly any, not many, less than half, not a lot, not very many.

Positive and Negative Scales?

Just as orderings could be formed for the positive group using the tests like those in examples (3), (4), and (5), orderings between negative items can be formed:

(27) Hardly any people drank gin. In fact, none did.
(28) Not many people drank gin. In fact, hardly any did.

This could provide the basis for a scale of negative items, if items can be ordered and the orderings are transitive.

Functionally, a positive scale can be thought of as ordered from the weakest statements about a whole set (e.g. *a few people like ice-cream*) to the strongest statement about the whole set (*all people like ice-cream*). It would presumably be used when the communicator wishes to focus on *how many* is the case, relative to *all*. In contrast, the negative scale can be thought of as ordered from weakest statements about the null set (*not quite everyone does this*) to the strongest (*no one does this*). It would be used when the communicator wishes to focus on *how few* are the case, relative to *none*. Thus, scales based on pragmatic considerations can be thought of as being about strength of claim rather than being about number or proportions denoted. This is a very different perspective from the simple scale-mapping view explored in Chapter 2, which is not directly concerned with the strength of claim being made by communicators. Obviously the linguistic notion of scale depends upon being able to order quantifiers in terms of magnitude, but at the very least there is a clear functional difference between negative and positive expressions. Thus, even though expressions like *few* and *a few* might give roughly equivalent values in a psychometric scaling task, they obviously have the capacity to serve different functions. In the next section, we shall describe some experiments that have a bearing on this point.

EMPIRICAL WORK ON NEGATIVITY AND COMPREHENSION

Negativity is obviously an important aspect of quantifier meaning, as is quantity information, regardless of how crude and context-dependent the quantity information might be. The question arises whether when subjects encode quantified statements that appear to be simply conveying fuzzy or vague quantity information, negativity is in fact used in setting up meaning representations. Two experiments have a bearing on this question.

Memory for Quantifiers

Memory performance can be used to draw inferences about how quantified statements are coded in memory (see Holyoak & Glass, 1978, for an early example). Sanford, Moxey, and McGinley (in prep.) carried out a study to investigate whether people would remember numerical (percentage) information better than the same information presented using natural language quantifiers. In a further condition, only implicit quantification was used. The following example statements serve to illustrate the three conditions:

Percent: 15% of schools supported the scheme.
Quantifier: Few of the schools supported the scheme.
No quantifier: Schools did not support the scheme.

The quantified statements were incorporated into a single passage, and subjects read this and were given a surprise free-recall test. The object was to investigate differences between presentation modes, and also to investigate error patterns for the explicit quantifier condition to see if negativity or positivity was preserved when errors of commission occurred. If the quantified versions were easier to remember than the percentage condition, then this would bode ill for the simple theory that quantifiers (like numbers) are translated onto a simple scale. Furthermore, if the error pattern with quantifiers preserved negativity and positivity, then it would be clear that negativity is utilised in understanding. Of course, error patterns (confusion matrices) have a long tradition of being used to investigate the form in which information is stored in memory (e.g. Bransford, Barclay, & Franks, 1972; Clark & Stafford, 1969; Conrad, 1964).

Each passage was presented to separate groups of subjects, in either printed or pre-recorded spoken form, making a total of six conditions. Subjects were told to read/listen to the passage, and that they would have to answer some questions afterwards. After presentation (or at the end of self-paced reading) they were given a surprise free-recall test. The passage was broken down into scoring-units, corresponding roughly to small complexes of propositions (Kintsch, 1974). In the case of a quantified statement (unit), they were further broken down into quantifier, remainder noun-phrase, and predicate. In scoring, we considered a proposition to be remembered if the remainder noun-phrase and the predicate were remembered. In other words, this score does not take into account whether the quantifier/percentage was correctly recalled. As the data in Table 3.1 show, there was a reliable effect of condition, with the natural language quantifier (NLQ) condition producing the best results, percentage condition (PC) the poorest results, and implicit quantification in the middle. These differences are statistically reliable.

If a remainder noun-phrase plus predicate combination is recalled, then it is possible that the quantifier was recalled correctly too. The percentage correct recall for the natural language quantifier and percentage groups are shown in row 2 of Table 3.1. The percentages were remembered correctly on reliably more occasions than natural language quantifiers.

TABLE 3.1
Average Recall of Material presented in each of the
Six Experimental Conditions

	Written Presentation			Auditory Presentation		
	NLQ	Implicit	PC	NLQ	Implicit	PC
Average idea unit	66%	64%	62%	63%	51%	40%
Average determiner recall	24%	–	58%	16%	–	37%

First row, average idea unit recall. Second row, average literal recall of determiner (not applicable to the implicit condition). See text for an explanation of these categories.

This is not such a strange state of affairs as might be supposed: There were simply more errors of commission for natural language quantifiers (55% of all errors) than for percentages (11% of all errors). However, the natural language quantifier errors were not random, nor within-text confusions; rather, there were several quite systematic aspects of the confusion matrix (Table 3.2).

One striking feature is that when items are misremembered, the erroneous recalls tend to belong to the same negative/positive group as the original item. That is, *not many* is more likely to be misremembered as *few* (another negative quantifier) than as *a few* (which is positive), whereas *few* is not likely to be misremembered as *a few*. Another prevalent type of error is the generalisation, in which negative expressions may be remembered as *none* (or *no*) generalisation, e.g. "Teachers don't like the method", and positive expressions may be remembered as generalisations such as "Teachers like the method". As we have already noted, the writers of such statements are not necessarily anticipating a truly universal interpretation.

Although literal percentages are remembered better than literal quantifiers, the use of percentages is not without its cost. In terms of the amount of material recalled overall, the use of natural language quantifiers gives superior performance. This could be for a number of reasons. For example, it may take more work on the part of readers to process and retain percentage statements, thus reducing retention as a whole. Indeed, in a follow-up study using a self-paced reading procedure, subjects were found to read sentences containing percentage statements more slowly than other ones, which to some extent offset the memory deficit. It is also likely that textual coherence is increased by the use of natural language expressions. This would certainly be in line with the argument that quantifiers work through structuring inferential activity, a point further explored in subsequent chapters. The fact that negativity is preserved in the confusion matrix indicates that negativity is probably the key in how quantifiers are understood.

TABLE 3.2
Confusions made between Natural Language Quantifiers in the Recall of Subjects in the Natural Language Quantifier Condition

			Quantifier Presented					
	most	many	quite a lot	quite a few	a few	only a few	few	hardly any
most	8	1	22	2				
many	9	5	5	6		1		
a lot	3	1		1				
quite a few								1
some	5		7			11		
a few	1			3	20	7		
only a few				1		5	1	1
+ve gen	8		14		6			
few					1	1	4	2
not many							2	
very few							3	1
most don't							2	
many don't							1	
not all						1		
–ve gen							8	4
forgot	6/40	19/40	13/40	12/40	19/40	14/40	19/40	21/40

The leftmost column is labelled *Quantifier recalled*.

+ve gen indicates a positive generalisation, such as "colleges are ..."; –ve gen indicates a negative generalisation, such as "colleges are not ...".

These ideas are subject to continuing investigation, but it is clear that percentages are more difficult to process than natural language quantifiers. As it is difficult to see how the translation of a percentage onto an internal scale could be more difficult than the translation of a vague quantifier, the results bode ill for a theory that assumes that percentages and quantifiers alike map onto a common internal scale.

Comparing Statements with the World

A particulary dramatic illustration of the influence of negativity on the comprehension of quantifiers comes from Just and Carpenter (1971) and Clark (1976). The task was to relate quantified statements to the verification of diagrams: Subjects were shown a sentence like *many of the dots are red* and asked to determine whether or not a diagram corresponded to this state of affairs, and the results suggested that the verification strategy depended upon negativity. In fact, it is clearly established that in a variety of tasks where the truth of sentences has to be evaluated, negative sentences take longer to evaluate than positive sentences (e.g. Clark, 1969; Gough, 1965, 1966; Wason & Jones, 1963). For example, (29) takes longer to evaluate than (30):

(29) Seven is not an even number.
(30) Eight is an even number.

Just and Carpenter (1971) set out to discover whether the same was true of negatives as they appear in different types of quantified sentence. They had subjects evaluate the truth or falsity of statements against pictures that consisted of 4 × 4 arrays of dots where each dot could be red or black. Sentences included explicitly signalled universal negatives (such as *None of the dots are red*, or *There are no red dots*), and corresponding affirmatives, such as *The dots are red*, and *There are red dots*. For nonuniversal statements, contrasts were made between affirmatives (e.g. *Many of the dots are red*), and negatives (e.g. *Few of the dots are red*). Finally, contrasts were made between what they term "semantic" affirmatives (e.g. *A majority of the dots are red*) and negatives (e.g. *A minority of the dots are red*). In a typical trial, a sentence was presented paired with a picture, and the match had to be evaluated. Thus, *A minority of the dots are red*, paired with 2 red and 14 black dots, would be true, but paired with 14 red and 2 black dots would be false. Both negative types took longer to evaluate than their positive counterparts, but differences were observed between the implicit negatives, such as *few of (X)*, and the "semantic" negatives, such as *a minority of (X)*. The difference turned out to be due to the way in which the subjects visualised the problem. Thus, for *a minority of (X)*, subjects coded the displays in terms of the *smaller subset*. However, for *few (X)*, subjects encoded in terms of the *majority subset*, the same one as is used for encoding *many of the (X)*. These results are interesting, because they show that positive and negative quantifiers induce different patterns of evaluating referent situations. We believe this pattern to have considerable psychological significance.

An explanation of these observations given by Clark (1976) uses ideas about negativity additional to those introduced earlier. If someone says *Helen isn't home*, there is what Clark calls a "supposition" that someone believes she is home: It is when there is reason to believe that such a supposition is made that an utterance containing such a negative could be made felicitously (see Wason, 1965). Clark extends this idea to negative quantifiers (with negativity analysed on the basis of Klima's work), supposing that when a negative statement such as *Few of the dots are red* is made, this has a semantic representation something like *it is false to suppose that the dots which are red are many*. Clark proposed that when the world is checked in order to test the truth of an utterance, the percept is coded in terms of the supposition. So, in the case above, the supposition causes subjects to check whether the dots are many, and so encoding is in terms of the majority number of dots. Clark's analysis of *A few of the dots are red* is something like: *It is correct to suppose that the number of dots that are red is small*. In this case, visual checking on the basis of the supposition is in terms of the minority number of dots. This analysis corresponds to the pattern observed in the data, of course, and also fits Clark's general model of verification. It constitutes strong behavioural evidence for the role of negativity in understanding what a quantifier is asserting.

GENERAL DISCUSSION

The psychological evidence for an explanation of quantifier meaning in terms of a mapping from expressions to some sort of internal scale is mixed. There is reasonable evidence that an ordinal scale can be created from a sets of quantifiers by a given individual. Yet with an independent-groups design, it is apparent that some quantifiers cannot really be differentiated in terms of the amounts they denote. The strong evidence for contextual dependency is also a problem for the scale-mapping idea as baseline assumptions may vary from individual to individual in some situations. Add to this the observations of high degrees of overlap among the values assigned to even quite small sets of quantifiers, and it becomes very implausible to suppose that more than a few quantifiers can really be sensibly distinguished from one another with respect to the expression-to-scale-mapping theory.

It is important to distinguish between the aforementioned claim and the idea that quantifiers cannot be distinguished in terms of scale values in a comparative setting. Consider the following interaction:

John: Few of the fans turned up at the match then?
Mary: Very few. We were all disappointed.

By using *very few*, Mary is asserting that the number was less than *few*. Linguistically, *very few* is a stronger statement in the direction of no fans turning up than is *few*.Thus, everyone agrees that *very few* is less than *few*: The point is that unless they specifically discuss the issue, there is no reason to suppose that John and Mary share common scale values for *few* and *very few* (the data in Chapter 2 suggests this is impossible). The difference between these expressions is in the strength of the claim being made about the smallness of the number of fans at the match. It is the linguistic notion of strength of claim that seems to provide the more realistic assessment of the scale meaning of the quantifiers.

This example illustrates a second point. It is possible to imagine a negative scale in that quantifiers can make differentially strong assertions about the smallness of proportions or quantities, and this possibility is associated with negative quantifiers. Quantifiers good for assertions about smallness were shown earlier to be different from those that are good for assertions about largeness. Experimental data from both memory studies and from picture–sentence verification shows that negative quantifiers are coded differently from positive ones in memory, and that they engender different picture-scanning procedures, so on these grounds alone it is evident that all quantifiers cannot be lumped together.

There are a number of elements in our discussion to be amalgamated. First, quantifiers are not necessarily discriminable in terms of the proportions they denote: Scaling studies show that if even a small number of expressions are scaled, there will be considerable overlap. We suggest that if a simple quantified assertion is made, then it will certainly not be given a numerical value, and that any mapping onto an internal scale will be coarse-grained. Rather, we believe that in noncomparative settings, quantifiers map onto aspects of situations that are associated with quantitative criteria. For instance, in the case of a party, *many* being there fits there being more than a criterion amount for it to be successful, or even for overcrowding, whereas *few* fits there being less than the criterion amount for this, but rather fits with too small a number to be successful, for instance. This can be achieved by a simple semantics in which there is a set of quantifiers that fit above some critical criterion, and a set that fit below, without the need for real numerical values at all. What counts is the inferences that are enabled by the expression. What happens with modified quantifiers (*quite a lot*, *very many*) will depend on how differentiable possible inferences are based on general knowledge about the situations in question. Thus, *very many people at a party* allows for a very successful party, or one which is overcrowded; the latter possibility emerges because the desirable number of people at a party has also an upper limit. On the other hand, whether *many* or *very many* is used in *many students passed their exams* is possibly immaterial to what inferences will be drawn, because there is no obvious upper limit to the critical criterion. However, an upper limit might come into play if there was reason to suppose that there was corruption in the examination process.

Much remains to be done to explore this line of reasoning, and it is clearly as much a problem of knowledge organisation as it is a problem of quantifiers *per se*. We are not claiming that this picture is completely justified; rather, our intention is to put forward a viable alternative to the psychometric account. In our alternative, how differentiable a quantifier turns out to be depends on how differentiable the inference patterns are that a scenario allows. We have indicated how there may be no need to give a numerical value or range interpretation of utterances containing quantifiers, and how comparative statements may be thought of in terms of strength of assertion. With expressions like *a significant number*, it is difficult to find any other way of thinking about its meaning.

Such an approach leads us away from scale-mapping as a way of trying to explain the large number of quantifiers from which we can choose, and to look for differentiations in terms of the effect they have on patterns of inferential activity. As a start, we have illustrated how quantifiers may be considered as strong or weak negative or positive statements. Negativity was shown to be preserved in memory representations of quantified statements, and to influence the pattern of encoding in sentence–picture comparisons. There has been relatively little psychological work on the way in which quantifiers might influence inference patterns, however. The remaining chapters of the book seek to rectify that position with a few simple studies.

NOTES

1. A problem with scaling by entailment is that the null set is not entailed by other quantifiers. So, it is unreasonable to say that *many men like the sun* entails *no men like the sun* (see e.g. Hirschberg, 1985, for a discussion). Also, entailment can be thought of in terms of strength of claim made in an utterance rather than in terms of set inclusion. Thus, if the objective is to make a claim relative to the universality of men being bald, then obviously *all men, many men,* and *some men* form an ordered set in terms of strength of claim, which is descending (see Harnish, 1979).
2. Acceptability of utterances is widely taken as a baseline for discussions about issues in semantics and pragmatics. The psychologist must ask the question "what is the process by which the judgements are made?" The suggestions we give here are hypothetical, given the absence of data. The theme of what process underlies semantic acceptability judgements will re-emerge from time to time.
3. This may sound a little strained because the gap between *a few*, at the very low end of the scale, and *all*, is so great. However, the strain is minimal when compared with the items (12)–(14)
4. Negative polarity items have a wide distribution over lexical types, encompassing such items as "bat an eyelid": Compare *not many/many people* batted an eyelid (see Seuren, 1985; Zwarts, 1991). Here we use them simply as diagnostics for classification.

CHAPTER FOUR

Focus and Attention Control

This chapter continues the exploration of the role of negativity in the interpretation of quantified statements. Our basic claims are that different quantifiers bring about different inferential patterns, and may be distinguished in terms of the subsets of the logical model upon which they focus.

ACCESSIBILITY, FOCUS, AND THINKING

Any quantified statement can be described in terms of sets, and our claim is that different quantifiers may serve to draw attention to different sets. By attention, we mean that one subset can be given priority in processing over others, and this subset will form the basis for inferences that will be drawn. In the preceding chapter a little evidence in favour of this idea was found in the work of Just and Carpenter (1971) and Clark (1976), in the patterns of verification times obtained when sentences and pictures were checked against one another. Here we make a more general claim that quantifiers control patterns of inference. The argument can be illustrated by reference to the familiar quantifier *some*.

Some and its Subsets

In the logical analysis of quantification, the term *some* has played a central role. In order to reason effectively with *some* (as in *some X are Y*), we have to take into account the following sets:

Set A The necessary existence of at least one X that is Y.
Set B The possible existence of Xs that are not Y.
Set C The possible existence of Ys that are not X.

Without taking into account all three of these elements, it is impossible to draw valid inferences on the basis of *some*. But are each of these sets of similar status in processing? For instance, intuitively, set C seems to be a less subjectively relevant aspect of what *some X are Y* asserts than the other two sets, even though all are essential for effective logical reasoning. Our idea is that in the face of an assertion, some aspects of the model will dominate processing more than others; that is, some things will tend to be in attentional focus, while others will not. In the present case, the question is which of the sets A, B or C will be in focus, and which will not.

The present use of the term focus may be operationally tied to the observation that some discourse entities seem to be easier to refer to by subsequent expressions than others. This sense of focus has been especially well studied in both linguistic (e.g. Ariel, 1990; Chafe, 1972; Grosz, 1977) and psychological frameworks (Garrod & Sanford, 1982; Sanford & Garrod, 1981).[1] Specifically, focus can be inferred through ease of pronominal reference. Because personal pronouns such as *it, she,* and *they* carry only minimal information to recover the referent (e.g. singular/plural; male/female/unmarked), it is clear that in practice things in a discourse that can be referred to by pronouns must be only a small subset of the possible previous antecedents, otherwise ambiguity would be rife. For this reason, focus has become closely associated with the conditions of felicitous pronominal anaphora, an idea most clearly expressed by Chafe (1972). In psychological studies, determinants of focus have been inferred from the ease of pronominal reference in reading time and judgement studies. Variables that influence the ease of pronominal reference include whether a noun phrase denotes an agent (Hudson, Tannenhaus, & Dell, 1986; Purkiss, 1978), whether the noun-phrase is the thematic subject or main character of a narrative (Garrod & Sanford, 1988; Marslen-Wilson, Levy, & Tyler, 1982), whether the description is a proper name (Sanford, Moar, & Garrod, 1988), whether the entity in question is mentioned early or late in a sentence (Gernsbacher, Hargreaves, & Beeman, 1989) and whether the entities being referred to are strongly related to currently active background knowledge (Anderson, Garrod, & Sanford, 1983). For the present purpose, the point is that pronouns are good for referring to things in focus, while noun-phrases of a more complex and informative kind are best for things not in focus. In this way, ease or acceptability of pronominal reference can be used as an index and a probe for the state of focus, other things being equal.

To see the use of such an analysis in building up a picture of the functions of quantifiers, consider the simple case of (1):

(1) Some lecturers are fast talkers.

What forms of reference can be used to address the three parts of the logical model, sets A, B, and C introduced earlier? First, using the pronoun *they* (which should address any set in focus), the following happens:

(2) They should slow down for introductory classes.[OK] set A
(3) They should speed up to be less boring.[*] set B
(The [*] indicates that (3) is unacceptable in the context of (1).)

Intuitively, whereas (2) is acceptable, (3) is not. Possibly (3) does not appear to make sense because *they* seems to refer to the subset of lecturers who are fast talkers (set A), but the predicate only makes sense with respect to the subset whose members are not fast talkers (set B). This kind of intuitive evidence suggests that the most accessible subset for reference is the set of lecturers who are fast talkers.

In order to better address the subset that is not in focus it is necessary to use something like the overtly contrastive expression *those who are not:*

(1) Some lecturers are fast talkers.
(4) Those who are not should speed up to be less boring.

(4) seems to be a good way to address the subset of which the predicate is not true (set B, exemplified by (4)). What about set C? In the present context, set C is that of fast talkers who are not lecturers. Neither *they* nor *those who are not* will address this subset. Indeed, this third subset has to be spelled out fully to be addressed:

(1) Some lecturers are fast talkers.
(5) The fast talkers who are not lecturers find them serious competition at dinner-parties.

In (5), the expression *The fast talkers who are not lecturers* serves to single out set C, but note that the pronoun *them* singles out set A, as before.

Therefore, for the quantifier *some*, the subset in focus seems to be set A, the necessary subset of which the predicate is true. Let us call this the normal reference set, or "refset", as it turns out to be the set that is normally in focus for most quantifiers. The other subsets are readily addressed only by more complex, informative expressions, with set B being accessible by simpler expressions than set C.

COMPSET FOCUS

Not all quantifiers have the same focus pattern as *some*. Take *not many*, for example. Application of the focus test using *they* produces the following pattern:

(6) Not many of the lecturers are fast talkers.
(7) They should slow down for the introductory classes.[?]
(8) They should speed up to be less boring.[OK]

The authors' intuitions are to the effect that (7) sounds somewhat infelicitous while (8) sounds fine. But note that in (8), *they* appears to pick up the group who are not fast talkers. Thus, it looks as though *not many* may be able to invoke a focal bias in the direction of the complement of the refset (the compset), or set B in the framework discussed. So it is perhaps possible to use a pronoun to refer to set B in this case. Other examples show that pronominal references to set B can be quite acceptable, but really strained for set A.

Of course, production of single examples does not give us the means to generalise about focus patterns. In some cases, it may be possible to find counter examples that do not fit the observation made earlier. For instance, the following example with *few* has *they* referring to the refset:

(9) Few students attended the meeting. They soldiered on with it anyway.

Therefore, rather than test our observations by having subjects check the acceptability of examples, a task was used in which preferences for compset or refset could be inferred from what subjects wrote in a continuation task. The number of quantifiers examined in this way has grown over a series of studies. The initial choice, however, was guided by the intuition that negative quantifiers seemed to be potentially compset licensing.

Empirical Evidence of Compset Focus

A series of experiments was carried out (Moxey & Sanford, 1987; Moxey, Sanford, & Barton, 1990; Sanford, Moxey, & McGinley, in prep.) in which each subject was presented with a sentence consisting of a quantified satement. A second sentence began with the plural pronoun *They*, followed by a blank, and subjects were asked to continue the sentence in a way that made a sensible continuation. A given subject only ever completed one such continuation. The object was to see whether the subjects used *they* to single out the refset, compset, or any other, and whether these tendencies were a function of quantifier. On the basis of initial experimenter intuitions, seven quantifiers were used in the initial studies: *hardly any, very few, few, not many, only a few, a few,* and *many*. The quantifiers were combined with two statements:

[Quantifier] of the MPs[2] were at the meeting. They ...
or
[Quantifier] of the football fans were at the match. They ...

After producing a continuation, each subject was invited to indicate what the expression "they" in their own continuation referred to, out of the following choice set:

MPs/Football fans in general
All MPs/Football fans
MPs/Football fans who went to the match
MPs/Football fans who didn't go to the match
Other (please state)

In 98% of cases, subjects' statements about their own foci of reference agreed with the opinions of two independent judges who checked all of the continuations produced. Figure 4.1 shows the proportion of uses of "they" judged as being compset as a function of quantifier. It also shows the results of a similar experiment in which the connective *because* was used: i.e. subjects had to complete sentences like:

(10) Few MPs attended the meeting because they ...

This was part of a manipulation of a number of connectives, described more fully in Moxey and Sanford (1987). It is clear that compset references occur, and that they appear to occur more frequently for some quantifiers than for others, and that their prevalence is amplified by the presence of *because*.

The tendency to produce compset references is just that: a tendency. For example, with *few*, the effect only occurs about 60% of the time, although this is amplified by *because*. So, when a quantifier is associated with a compset, it is not a strict requirement, but an option. It is better to say that some quantifiers are compset licensing, because they allow but do not require compset references. But notice that *many* never produced a compset, and *a few* did so on only one occasion. It is therefore possible that these quantifiers effectively preclude compset references. This asymmetry is reflected in the relative ease with which felicitous refset references can

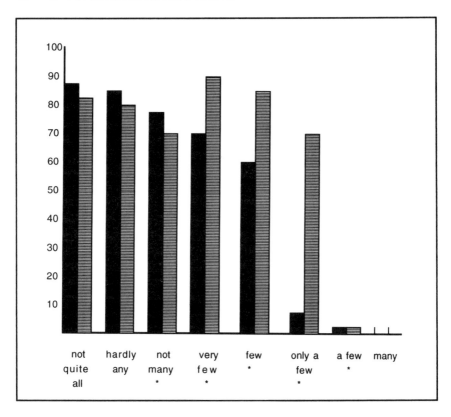

FIG. 4.1. Proportion of compset references in the continuations. Solid bars: full-stop condition. Hatched bars: "because" condition. (Cases marked * from Moxey & Sanford, 1987; others from Sanford, Moxey, & McGinley, in prep.).

be found for compset-licensing quantifiers, and the difficulty (one might say effective impossibility) of finding felicitous compset references for those that appear not to license compsets. The expression *only a few* is curious, in that the likelihood of a compset is almost zero in the absence of *because*, but is quite high in the presence of *because*. On the present data, it seems to lie between obvious refset focusers and compset focusers: It is weakly compset licensing. We shall have more to say about compset focusing after *only a few* shortly.

Another thing worthy of note is the way in which *very few* produces a higher proportion of compset references than *few*: Although this effect is very small, it is reliable. The usual way of thinking about the action of *very* on a quantifier is that it exaggerates the position of the determiner on a scale (*very few* is fewer than *few*; *very many* is more than *many*), but these results show that *very* intensifies the tendency towards compset focus.

Earlier we suggested that *very few* is simply an amplified version of *few*: Whatever inferences follow in the train of using *few*, *very few* indicates an amplification. Here there is at least some evidence for an amplification of the occurrence of compsets.

Although such combinations of quantified sentence and pronoun do occur naturally in real text, they are rare. It would be misleading to leave the reader with any other impression. However, our intention was to probe focus through the pronouns. Some data collected by Moxey (reported in Moxey et al., 1990) suggest that when free continuations are obtained, in which there is no connective, and no pronoun to head the continuation, then results are broadly consistent with the picture painted here.

Compset's Nature

While the occurrence of compset cases was both identified by the subjects themselves as the set they intended *they* to refer to, and agreed independently (and blindly) by at least two judges, there is still a possible ambiguity in the strict acceptance of compset reference. Consider the following example, taken from the data:

(11) Few of the MPs were at the meeting. They were too busy.

An alternative to the strict compset hypothesis is that *they* in these cases stands for *MPs in general*. The essence of this argument is that we could rewrite (11) as something like (12), where the brackets contain elided material:

(12) They were (all) too busy to attend (but one or two went anyway).

Several specific versions of this idea are possible, ranging from the elided version to versions meaning *too busy in general*, or *typically too busy*. The surface plausibility of such a view finds support in our previous observations that statements having the form of generalisations are seldom to be interpreted as truly universal generalisations. One theoretical motivation for doubting compset reference as a strict binding of pronoun to compset is that in a number of theories of the structure of discourse that deal with quantification (notably Kamp's (1984) Discourse Representation Theory), anaphoric pronominal reference is restricted either to the superset of a quantified statement, or to the refset. So, if we want to consider the pronoun anaphoric within the theory, the whole-set interpretation is preferable.

However, there are problems with the idea that compset references are generalisations. First, subjects had the opportunity of checking *MPs in general*, or *all MPs*, and simply chose not to do so. Independent judges behaved in the same way, and it is hard to see why there is a misunderstanding over the intended referent. The fact is that both subjects and independent readers believe that compset references are made and that they are intended to be made. (However, we have known critics to argue that subjects simply do not know what they mean by *they*, and that the references are really to things "in general".) However, a second reason for supposing that the compset is being referred to is that there are many instances in the data of continuations ending with the expression *instead*, for instance:

(13) Hardly any of the MPs attended the meeting. They were out at the pub or with their secretaries instead.

The use of *instead* serves to single out those who acted in a way other than by going to the meeting, and that is the compset.[3]

A final line of argument relies upon a recent study by Sanford et al. (in prep.), in which continuation tests were carried out using the complex expression *not quite all*. If *not quite all MPs went to the meeting*, then clearly most did, so this expression denotes a (very) high proportion. Yet the predominant continuation type was the compset (at 88%), as indexed by our usual operational criterion of what the subjects thought they were referring to:

(14) Not quite all of the MPs were at the meeting.
(15) They stayed at home instead.

Clearly, *they* cannot in any sense mean *MPs in general*, because it is the small, exceptional group that stayed at home. This is a clear argument against the view that compset references are somehow generalisations about the superset, and therefore we reject the view that any theoretical treatment supposing this to be the case would be useful.[4]

The sentence–picture verification work of Just and Carpenter (1971) provides other evidence for the kind of attentional bias we are claiming. Recall that when confronted with the sentence *Not many of the dots are black*, subjects chose to check the picture in terms of the red dots. This is a clear behavioural concomitant of compset focus.

One possible reason for the reluctance on the part of some researchers to accept that certain quantifiers lead to compset focus is the fact that the compset is defined merely as the complement of the refset. This is a vague, complicated definition, because to specify the complement of a set one must first identify the set and then discover its complement. In some instances the text alone will not unambiguously determine the complement of a mentioned set. For example, *few carol singers came to my door last night* has a clear refset (the set of carol singers who came to my door). The complement of this set might be, for example, (a) all of those carol singers who didn't come to my door, (b) those carol singers I thought might come to my door last night, but didn't, or even (c) those people who came to my door last night who were not carol singers. The use of the restricting construction *of the*, as in *few of the carol singers*, rules out some complement sets, (c) for example, and this is why our subjects were presented with expressions taking the form *Q of the S*. In everyday language we might assume that contextual constraints rule out all but one relevant complement, or indeed that in many situations *any* of the complements would do. The latter argument is akin to the possibility that language users do not completely resolve the referent of *it* in *He wanted a Hitachi radio. It was in Fraser's window*. The pronoun *It* might refer to a particular radio, or any one of a number of radios. The exact referent is not necessary in order for the reader to make the appropriate set of inferences (Sanford & Garrod, 1989). Nevertheless, the more we can tie down the process of identifying the compset in general, the more acceptable and useful it will be as a concept. One way of tying it down is to see if it is associated in any way with formal, well-defined categories. In other words, do compset quantifiers have other distinguishing properties that might explain or at least constrain their definition? We shall discuss this shortly. First, we turn to a discussion of the content of the continuations.

INFERENTIAL ACTIVITY: THE CONTENT OF FOCUS

The focus patterns described have been discussed up to now in terms of the aspect (or subset) of the logical model that seems to be most available for pronominal reference. But an analysis of the content of the continuations produced serves to show us more detail of what kind of interpretations are actually given to the quantified statements themselves, and to what types of patterns of inference this might lead. Moxey (1986) noted that the continuations seemed to convey readily classifiable sorts of information, and developed a classification scheme that was applied to the continuations of all of the studies described here. The least interesting type of continuation simply described some detail of what happened next, given a quantified statement:

(16) Only a few of the fans went to the match. They rioted on the way home because the team lost again.

But some of the continuations seemed to be more like comments on the way the quantifier divided the set. The most common of these give a reason for not going to the match/meeting:

(17) Few of the fans went to the match. They didn't want to be embarrassed yet again by the team's bad performance.

Such continuations may be termed "reasons why the predicate is not true of the refset", reason-why-not (RWN), for short. Similarly, another type of continuation might be termed reason-why (RW), explaining why, in the present case, the fans did go to the match:

(18) A few of the fans went to the match. They wanted to see United win for once.

These continuation types are of interest because they indicate a potential explanation for why subjects might want to focus on one or other subset. A fourth type of continuation is also interesting in this respect, indicating a consequence (cons) of the proportion denoted by the quantifier:

(19) Only a few of the fans went to the match. They cheered louder than usual to make up for their lack of numbers.

In order to investigate the prevalence of these types of continuation, six independent judges examined each and every one of the continuations produced in our study, and used a classification scheme based on the types described earlier. Agreement was high, and the outcome of the judgements is shown in Table 4.1

What is most noteworthy is that *a few* leads to continuations that are of the next-event variety, and not to continuations that are in any way a comment based on the way the quantifier divides the set. In complete contrast, *few*, *not many*, *very few*, and *hardly any* cause most subjects to concentrate on RWN, this tendency correlating well with compset reference.

The expression *only a few* is interesting in that it fits neither pattern. Rather, there were two dominant types of continuation: The first being the next-event type which follows *a few* and *many*; and the second being reasons for the small number attending. This pattern identifies *only a few* as signalling a comment on the small number (unlike *a few*), but as not focusing on reasons why a large number did not attend, a property of the compset-licensing quantifiers. As we saw in the section Compset Focus, however, the behaviour of this expression is complicated. When the connective *because* is used with *only a few*, compset continuations occur, and from Table 4.1 it is clear that RWN continuations occur in parallel. So is the compset-licensing feature dependent on the need to give a RWN-type continuation? If a speaker wanted to make an assertion about RWN, and was forced to use a pronoun, then compset reference could certainly be the result.

TABLE 4.1
Continuation Type based on Judges' Responses

Expression	Dominant	Secondary
A few	WHN[1]	RW
A few because	RW	—[2]
Only a few	WHN/RW	—
Only a few because	RWN	RW
Not many	RWN	—
Not many because	RWN	—
Few	RWN	WHN
Few because	RWN	—
Very few	RWN	
Very few because	RWN	
Many	WHN	RW
Many because	RW	—
Not quite all	RWN	—
Not quite all because	RWN	—
Hardly any	RWN	—
Hardly any because	RWN	—

[1] What Happened Next
[2] '—' indicates that there is no secondary response type, because the dominant type includes all or almost all of the continuations.
   The first group are from Moxey and Sanford (1987), based on the responses of six independent judges. For further numerical details, see Moxey and Sanford. The second group are from the study of Sanford, Moxey, and McGinley (in prep.), and are from agreed classifications by two independent judges. Only the dominant and secondary continuation types are indicated for simplicity.

Attractive though this idea is, there is some evidence suggesting that compset reference is not necessarily (solely and directly) dependent on RWN continuations. Reasons are normally given for states of affairs that are exceptional: If a state of affairs is unexceptional, then normally there will be no perceived reason to comment on it. (See e.g. Turnbull, 1986, or Hilton and Slugoski, 1986, for a discussion of this idea.) By using a context in which the state of affairs denoted by the propositional content of a statement does not violate a norm, Moxey and Sanford (1987) were able to show that compset reference does not depend on explanation-giving. An example completed continuation is shown in (20):

(20) Few of the children hated Santa Claus. They left him plenty of milk and cookies.

The normal state of affairs is for children to like Santa Claus so there should be no tendency for people to explain why the large compset of children like Santa Claus. Indeed, the results of the experiment showed a high number of compset references, but very few reason-continuations, as exemplified by (20). This is not to say that the need to produce RWN continuations does *not* lead to compset references, of course.

DISCUSSION

Negative quantifiers allow patterns of focus that are not allowed by positive quantifiers, as defined in Chapter 3. We have termed them compset licensing, and have produced evidence that suggests that they are not generalisations (superset references), certainly not all of them. Closely associated with the (referentially indexed) focus pattern are patterns of continuation showing a focus on different inferential activities (reasons for the predicate to be false, or RWN; reasons for it to be true, or RW, and consequences of the small number). If it is assumed that both situations used in the experiment (MPs attending a meeting and fans attending a match) lead subjects to expect high attendance, the negative quantifiers may lead to RWN because of the violation between the small amount described and the large amount expected. With the exception of *a few*, the positive quantifiers do not lead to a violation and therefore no reason or explanation should be expected. The fact that *a few* does not lead subjects to produce reasons leads us to believe that there is some (not necessarily logical) link between negative quantifiers and RWN continuations that goes beyond the link between norm violation and explanation-giving. If the situations presented had been such that a low number was the norm (e.g. the number of children hating Santa Claus), then it remains to be seen whether positive quantifiers lead to reasons. It is clear that if a norm is violated, an explanation is required. We suspect also that negative quantifiers suggest that a norm has been violated in situations where other sources of information remain unclear on this point. For example, it seems most likely that the norm for MPs attending meetings is not clearly high or low, but that the presence of a negative quantifier to describe the proportion attending indicates that a high proportion should be taken as the norm. Thus the strong correlation between negative quantifiers like *few* and RWN, whereas there is none between *a few* and RW in this context. Unless obviously false, negative quantifiers indicate a norm violation and then a RWN is desirable by way of explanation.

The expressions explored fall into three main groups.

A. The positives: *a few, many*. This small group produces only refset references, and simple (nonreason) continuations. We can say that they do not serve to make a comment on the number or proportion that they single out. We expect other positives to behave the same way, in general.

B. The negatives: *few, very few, not many, hardly any, not quite all.* These produce compsets and serve to signal a comment on the proportions or numbers that they single out to the effect that a violation has occurred. This then leads to RWN continuations.

C. *Only a few.* This expression is positive by some tests, such as a tag test: *Only a few people came, didn't they?*[OK]/*did they?*[not OK]. But it is negative (but uncomfortable) with a negative polarity item: *Only a few people believe in Santa anymore.* (For empirical evidence that it is uncomfortable with a negative polarity item, see Moxey and Sanford, 1987.) It is compset licensing when combined with the connective *because* it forces RWN, but otherwise seems to be biased to the refset, and induces consequences as its focal pattern.

In summary, the data presented here provide a means of differentiating among quantifiers in terms of the patterns of inferential activity that they predominantly induce. In the next chapter, we shall explore the possible origins of the compset-focusing property, examine other expressions that show the same kind of focus patterns, and discuss the relation of compset licensing to some logical and linguistic properties of quantifiers.

NOTES

1. Focus is one of those terms that have a variety of uses in the linguistic literature, and so its use in one sense can prove an irritation to those who would use it in a different sense. Our use is psychological in nature: We mean focus of attention in that certain aspects of a representation are given prominence within the processor. This will correlate with linguistic phenomena, of course, and so at various points will meet other definitions of focus head-on.
2. MPs: conventional way of describing Members of Parliament.
3. Even here, it may be possible to argue that it is MPs in general who are being talked about, but additional arguments would have to be brought to bear to explain why *instead* had been used.
4. Hans Kamp (personal communication) suggested that within his scheme of things, compset reference should be thought of as a kind of deixis rather than as anaphoric.

CHAPTER FIVE

Focus: Foundations and Extensions

In this chapter, a number of separate strands are considered that converge fully only at the end. We begin with a discussion of an important logical property of quantifiers we believe to be directly related to the compset-licensing property. We then look at other expressions (numeric, adverbs) that have compset licensing properties as well. We then discuss the possible basis for compset focus, and introduce a developmental study, which with other evidence suggests that compset can be induced in more than one way. Finally, we summarise the relation of compset to a variety of linguistic and judgmental phenomena.

PSYCHOLOGICAL AND LOGICO-LINGUISTIC PROPERTIES OF COMPSET FOCUSERS

With the exception of *only a few*, those quantifiers that produce compset patterns are negative. *Only a few* is negative in so far as it takes negative polarity items in simple declarative sentences, but it is not negative by a tag test. Indeed, our investigations lead us to believe that expressions taking negative polarity items in simple declaratives are compset-licencers. It is established that negative polarity items require that the quantifying expression with which they are combined be *monotone decreasing* (see Barwise & Cooper, 1981; Fauconnier, 1979, for seminal work; Ladusaw, 1979; also Zwarts, 1991, for a more recent view). If this is true, then any monotone decreasing expression should also be compset licensing. First, let us define monotone decreasing (mon dec) and monotone increasing (mon inc).

According to some classifications in logic, natural language quantifiers can be monotonic, or nonmonotonic.[1] The important point for us about monotonicity is that it specifies classes of inference that can be made on the basis of quantified expressions, and so has strong consequences for communication and reasoning. If quantifiers are monotonic, they can be mon inc or mon dec (see, for example, Barwise & Cooper, 1981; or Keenan & Stavi, 1986). Monotonicity is a formal mathematical property based on set-to-subset relations, but a natural language test that is used as a diagnostic for the property of mon inc is:

(1) If Q of the students sat the exam reluctantly, then Q of the students sat the exam.

Consider what this means for the quantifier *more than half of the students*:

(2) If more than half of the students sat the exam reluctantly, then more than half of the students sat the exam.

This seems to be automatically valid. If *more than half of the students* did X is true, and X is a proper subset of Y, then it is also true that *more than half of the students* did Y. This is what is meant by mon inc. Now consider *less than half of the students*:

(3) If less than half of the students sat the exam reluctantly, then less than half of the students sat the exam.

This is quite false. All of the students could have sat the exam, for instance. Therefore, this quantifier is not mon inc. The test for mon dec examines whether the truth of a statement about the superset (Y) necessitates the truth of a statement about a proper subset of Y:

(4) If Q of the students sat the exam, then Q of the students sat the exam reluctantly.

Substituting *less than half* for Q gives a valid result, which is thus shown to be mon dec. With *more than half*, the result is not valid.

To see how the property mon dec might be applied in everyday interactions, consider the following:

John: Did many people arrive at the party after midnight?
Mary: Not many people came to the *party*!

(If *not many people came to the party*, then *not many people came to the party after midnight*; if any did, *not many* is treated as though it were mon dec.) The reasoning, supported by the mon dec property, is concerned with reasoning from the superset to a proper subset.

Among formalists, opinions vary about which natural language quantifiers are mon inc or mon dec. Barwise and Cooper (1981) consider *many* to be mon inc and *few* to be mon dec. They are less sure about *a few*, but our own intuitions based on replacing Q in (2) with *a few* are that this expression is mon inc. Keenan and Stavi (1986) also class *a few* as mon inc. Unfortunately they only deal with quantifiers that they consider to be extensional, so that *many* and *few* are excluded from their analysis. Table 5.1 lists some mon dec, mon inc, and nonmonotonic quantifiers. Barwise and Cooper claim that all simple natural language quantifiers are monotone, either increasing or decreasing, (*exactly N* being nonmonotone, but a complex expression). Barwise and Cooper (1981) also say that

TABLE 5.1

(a): Determiners producing Monotone and Nonmonotone Quantifiers

Mon dec: no, neither, not one, at most 1, 2, 3 ... , only 1, 2, 3 ... , few, finitely many
Mon inc: all, each, every, at least *N*, the 1, 2, 3 ... , both, most, many, several
Nonmonotone: exactly, 1, 2, 3 ... , exactly X.

From Barwise & Cooper, 1981; Zwarts, 1991

(b): Results of an Experiment in which Judgements were made Using the Frame "If Q of the People Entered the Race, then Q of the People Entered the Race Early" (a test of mon dec)

Expression	Proportion Yes	Average Confidence (1 = sure, 5 = guess)
None	100%	1.0
Less than 10	100%	1.4
Few	100%	1.4
Not many	100%	2.4
Only a few	60%	3.2
A few	20%	2.6
All	0%	1.0
Some	0%	1.0

expressions that appear to be nonmonotone can be expressed as a conjoint of expressions that are monotone (for instance, *exactly five* could be thought of as being a conjunction of *not more than five* and *not less than five*). This is an important restriction on natural language. As they suggest, it is unlikely that any natural language would have a basic determiner corresponding to *an even number of*, or *all but one*, which are nonmonotone.

The prototype mon dec quantifier is *less than X* (or *X or less*, or *not more than X*), while the prototype mon inc is *more than X* (or *X or more*, or *not less than X*). The success of these expressions in tests of monotonicity is guaranteed deductively. This is not true of many other expressions, which have to be judged on a purely intuitive basis. We suggest that the judgement of an expression as mon dec or mon inc depends on how readily they are interpreted as *X or less* or *X or more*. So, if *few people* is taken to mean *X or less people*, then it will be judged as producing a valid result in frame (4), even though the result cannot be proven deductively. On this line of reasoning, the ease with which a mon dec interpretation is suggested by an expression will be a force towards an intuitive acceptance that it is mon dec in a linguistic test, whereas the extent to which other nonmonotonic or mon inc interpretations intrude will result in doubts about the "automatic validity" of the result.

Our hypothesis is that compset focusing provides the basis for the nondeductive judgement about monotonicity. The line of argument is as follows. Focusing on the compset requires that any inferences drawn will concern the compset and not the refset. Furthermore, inferences will concern *the largeness of the compset* (explaining it), so that any argument to the effect that the refset is extremely small (or indeed empty) will not affect the validity of inferences drawn. The refset is thus licensed as being treated as empty (but may not necessarily lead explicitly to this conclusion). This could account for the phenomenon of using *all* to describe the compset, illustrated by the following example:

(5) Few of the fans went to the football match. They all watched the game on television instead.

The use of *all* in this way is not uncommon in our data, yet it is slightly strange, because no subject supposes that few of the fans means none of the fans. Rather than considering this to be loose usage, it may be the case that when attention is fully on the compset, the refset is effectively empty. Indeed, as we showed in Chapter 3, the possibility of an empty set is not ruled out by compset licensing expressions:

(6) Few of the fans went to the match. In fact none did.

Thus, we propose that the *process* of compset focusing allows the null set, and allowing the null set provides the grounds for the interpretation *X or less* to hold. Thus, in a frame test for monotonicity, compset licencers will be mon dec, other things being equal, thus licensing the classes of inference possible with mon dec expressions, and allowing combination with negative polarity items.

As we might expect, in practice people have difficulty in making judgements of whether quantifiers are intuitively mon dec. In Table 5.1(b) we show the results of a small empirical study in which a variety of quantifiers were presented in the standard frame "If Q of the people entered the race, then Q of the people entered the race early". Student subjects were asked to judge the validity of this form when Q was varied. They were also asked to indicate on a scale of 1 (certain) to 5 (guess) how confident they were in the validity of their choices, and were invited to make comments if they wished to. Those quantifiers producing an analytically true result (*nobody* and *less than 10*) were given very high confidence and were universally claimed as valid. But *few* and *not many*, although judged to be valid, produced lower ratings. The expression *only a few* was judged as valid by some, and invalid by others, and produced low confidence scores. So, in this particular frame test, the judgement of mon dec seems to be an uncertain affair. Subjects' comments and post-test discussions proved illuminating. For example, one subject, judging *only a few* as mon dec, commented: "If only a few entered, then it is possible for a few to have entered early, though not necessarily all of these few did enter early". Clearly, the template *X or less* was in this subject's mind, even if he came down in favour of a possible rather than a deductive response. To the extent that *only a few* is automatically read as *X or less*, the test expression seems valid. For the expression *many people*, the same subject judged the result as invalid, but commented: "Should be the same logic as with only a few, but isn't (on first thought)". Comments of other subjects are consistent with this single example (Sanford & Moxey, 1991). We suggest that *many* is not interpretable as *X or less* because it is not compset focusing.

In their intuitive analysis, Barwise and Cooper (1981) suggest that any quantifier might be thought of as monotone, because a quantifying expression seems to be capable of being expressed as a conjunction of other quantifiers. Analysing *a few X* in this way, they suggest that it might be thought of being potentially translated into *some but not many X*. The second of this pair is of course mon dec. It seems that what we are suggesting about the extent to which an *X or less* interpretation is applicable to a quantifier is very much along the same lines, but is expressed more in terms of processing considerations.

Although one might claim that unless the results of suitable tests are deductively true they cannot be logically valid, the point is that the inclusion of many quantifiers in the framework of generalised quantifier theory by Barwise and Cooper (1981) requires an appeal to intuition (as Barwise and Cooper explicitly state). It is these intuitions that we try to explore here.

OTHER EXPRESSIONS THAT LICENSE COMPSET FOCUS

Numerical Expressions

Compset focus should be associated with expressions containing numbers only if they admit an empty-set interpretation. This should rule out compset reference with straight proportions, such as 5% of the MPs. Of course, the statement 5% of the MPs were at the meeting certainly implicates that 95% were not, so on more general grounds it might be supposed that compset reference might be possible. We suggest it will not. But hybrid expressions such as at most X% (or less than X%) are paragon examples of mon dec quantifiers, allowing the null set. Similarly, the expressions at least X% (or more than X%) are mon inc. We would predict that the mon dec hybrids would be compset licensing. Other hybrid expressions are much harder to guess, for example only 5%.

In a recent study, Sanford, Moxey, and McGinley (in prep.) tested the referential preferences associated with hybrids as well as simple percentages. The continuation method was used as before, and subjects indicated the intended referent of the plural pronoun. The results are shown in Table 5.2. For simple percentage statements, there is little evidence of compset licensing. Where X is a very low number, X% appears to behave like a few, even though 0.5% of A are B implies that 99.5% of A are not B. Hybrid statements of the form only X% of A seem to behave like only a few in that compset reference is licensed although far from preferred in the MPs/fans contexts, but the effect is amplified when the connective because is used. The results thus provide evidence of a link between monotonicity and compset licensing: Hybrid expressions containing less than are mon dec, and these are more likely than any other expressions in this hybrid study to produce compset reference.

Unlike natural language expressions such as few, not many, or hardly any, these hybrids explicitly allow a zero interpretation, and are thus mon dec. Natural language expressions allow zero interpretations only in circumstances where the inferences that the interpreter is intended to make are consistent with a zero interpretation, and this will be so if the inferences concern the compset. Hence the link between monotonicity and compset licensing is more coincidental for hybrid expressions in that both their monotonicity and their compset-licensing tendencies are a result of

TABLE 5.2
Set Referred to and Dominant Type of Continuation Resulting from the Use
of Percentage Statements

Expression	Set			Dominant Continuation
	Ref	Comp	Other	
10%	0.85	0.10	0.05	Other
5%	0.70	0.05	0.25	Other
2%	0.95	0.05	0.00	Other
0.5%	0.85	0.10	0.05	Other
10% because	0.90	0.00	0.10	RW
5% because	0.80	0.15	0.05	RW
2% because	0.90	0.10	0.00	RW
0.5% because	0.70	0.05	0.25	RW
Only 10%	0.75	0.125	0.125	RW/Other
Only 0.5%	0.80	0.20	0.00	RW/Other
Only 10% because	0.475	0.35	0.175	RWN/RW
Only 0.5% because	0.30	0.40	0.30	RWN
Less than 80%	0.575	0.375	0.05	RWN/Other
Less than 20%	0.325	0.625	0.05	RWN
Less than 80% because	0.15	0.70	0.15	RWN
Less than 20% because	0.075	0.775	0.15	RWN
More than 80%	0.95	0.00	0.05	RW
More than 20%	0.975	0.00	0.025	RW
More than 80% because	0.95	0.05	0.00	RW
More than 20% because	1.00	0.00	0.00	RW

RWN: reason for predicate to be false; RW: reason for it to be true.

the zero interpretation possibility. For the natural language expressions considered in previous studies, monotonicity depends on the zero interpretation possibility, which is in turn dependent on compset licensing.

Frequency Adverbs

Although our work has concentrated on quantifiers of amount, a parallel set of arguments can be made for frequency adverbs. Compare *often* and *occasionally* with *seldom, rarely*, and *only occasionally*, for instance. The first group will not combine with a negative polarity item, for example:

(7) Mary often eats at home anymore.[*]

but the second does, for example:

(8) Mary seldom eats at home anymore.[OK]

A parallel to the mon dec test produces a valid result for the second group too:

(9) If Mary seldom eats at home, then Mary seldom eats rice at home.

Frequency adverbs do not readily offer sentence frames in which plural pronouns can be used to probe focus, but the content of continuations can be compared with those found for the quantifiers. Moxey et al. (1990) investigated the continuations produced by subjects given materials such as:

(10) John [quantifier] goes to the cinema. He ...

Six judges classified the responses according to a pre-arranged scheme. The expressions *seldom* and *rarely* produced a response pattern dominated by reasons for not going (a parallel to the RWN responses with compset-licensing quantifiers). The term *only occasionally* produced reasons for not going and reasons for going in equal numbers. By itself, *occasionally* produced a very low incidence of "reason" continuations. We suggested the following correspondences:

a few = occasionally
only a few = only occasionally
few/very few = rarely/seldom

WHAT TRIGGERS COMPSET REFERENCE PATTERNS?

While compset reference is associated with negative quantifiers, there remains the case of *only a few* (and *only X%*), which yielded the compset pattern only when coupled with the connective *because*. We conjectured that compset focusing might be associated directly with negatives, this being the major origin of compset reference patterns. But they may also occur if RWN inference patterns are elicited by some other means. In the case of *only a few*, which has been shown to induce a search of explanations, if RWN are readily available, then compset reference might follow. Two lines of evidence relate to this conjecture. The first is developmental trends in compset focus, and the second, direct consideration of availability of information of the RWN type.

Developmental Trends in Compset Effects

If compset focusing is based on negativity, then one would expect that an explicit negative, such as *not many*, would be the first to show it developmentally, followed by implicit negatives such as *few*. Indirect routes to compset focus, requiring knowledge utilisation as well as an understanding of linguistic cues, might be expected to be even later in appearing: Thus, one might expect a late development of compset focusing to *only a few*. Apart from the general interest of tracking the developmental patterns of compset focusing, we hoped that a differential pattern would be obtained compatible with the dual process idea. It is based on the view that it would be unlikely (although possible) that two independent processes will be acquired at exactly the same time.

In an acquisition study (Moxey & Sanford, in prep.), subjects were asked to complete fragments such as this in a way which would make sense as part of a story:

[Quantifier] of the children ate their ice-cream. They ...

In the sentences presented to subjects [Quantifier] was replaced by one of the following: *not many, a few, only a few, many,* or *few*. This particular sentence was chosen because it has a similar structure to those used in the adult studies, yet the topic should make it fairly easy for younger children to think of sensible continuations of the text. Furthermore, expectations in general will be strong that children should like ice-cream, unlike the aforementioned work with MPs and football fans. This point turns out to be important. Subjects from four different age groups were tested: 8–10 years, 12 years, 15 years, and adults (older than 17 years). Within these age groups the subjects were divided into five independent groups, corresponding to the five quantifiers. All of the sentence continuations were passed to six independent judges, who were asked to indicate the subset to which the plural pronoun seemed to refer for each continuation.

Figure 5.1 shows the compset pattern as a function of age group and quantifier. The quantifier presented to subjects resulted in significantly different interpretations regardless of the age of subjects. More specifically, it is clear that in general, *not many* led subjects to focus on the compset significantly more than other quantifiers; *few* and *only a few* led subjects to focus on the compset equally and more than *a few* did. The age of the subject also significantly influenced the probability of focus on the compset

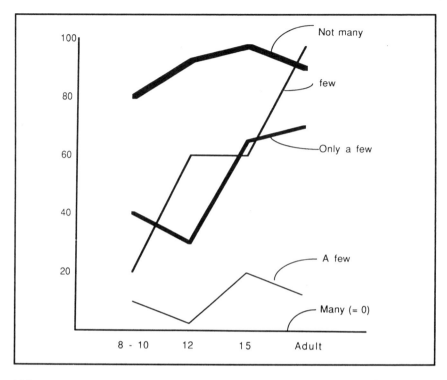

FIG. 5.1. Estimate of the proportion of compsets for five quantifiers in the responses of four age groups. (Data from Moxey & Sanford, in prep.)

regardless of the quantifier presented. Subjects 8 to 10 years old produced fewer compset references than 12-year-olds, as well as 15-year-olds and adults. Subjects aged 12 produced more compsets than 8–10-year-olds, but fewer than 15-year-olds as well as adults.

Turning to the interaction, the age of the subject only influenced interpretation with the quantifiers *only a few* and *few*. As Fig. 5.1 suggests, subjects almost always produce a compset reference after *not many*, but almost never after *a few*. But the probability of a compset reference after *few* or *only a few* clearly increases with age. When presented with *few*, 8–10-year-olds produced significantly fewer compsets than older subjects. Also 12- and 15-year-old subjects produced significantly fewer compsets after *few* than their adult counterparts. This result is illustrated in Fig. 5.1, where there is a clear increase in compset references between subjects aged 8–10 and 12, and between 15-year-olds and adult subjects. The only reliable difference in compset production after *only a few* is between 12 and 15 years. Thus, there appear to be three distinct changes in compset-producing behaviour dependent on the age of subjects: Between 10 and 12 years there is an increase in compsets after *few*; between 12 and 15 years there is an increase in compsets after *only a few*; and between 15 years and adult (minimum 17 years) there is a second increase in the frequency of compset references after *few*. The judges also placed the continuations in categories according to their content. Again, there was an overwhelming tendency for continuations that focus on the compset also to provide reasons for the negation of the predicate (RWNs).

The findings are broadly consistent with the view presented at the outset. Compset focus patterns are associated with explicit negatives early (8–10 years), with implicit negatives later (12 years), and occur through *only a few* much later (15 years). However, the increase in compset focus after *few* is in two stages. The first increase is between 8–10 years and 12 years, and this finding is consistent with the fact that *few* is implicitly negative, and with the view that this property is often discovered between these ages. The second increase in compset reference after *few* is between 15 years and adult. From this we might conclude that some of our subjects do not realise that *few* is negative until they are much older. Perhaps a better explanation is that *few* can lead us to focus on the compset for the same reason that *only a few* can. Subjects do not usually acquire the less direct association between *only a few* and compset focus until they are 15 years old and thus *few* cannot lead to compset focus via this association until later than this.

Availability of Knowledge Supporting Inference

Whereas (12) yields hardly any compset references, (13) yields them about two-thirds of the time:

(12) Only a few of the MPs were at the meeting.
(13) Only a few of the children ate their ice-cream.

Our current idea about this difference is in terms of the causal information contained in our background knowledge of the two situations. Continuations after *only a few* (and certain other quantifiers) tend to be explanations for the small number, e.g. why did so few MPs attend the meeting? In order to answer this sort of question we can either think of a reason why a small number attended (e.g. the MPs who were there were very dedicated [from this we might infer that the meeting was unusually trivial or boring]), or we can think of a reason why a large number did not or could not attend (e.g. the MPs who did not attend were busy in their constituencies).

Likewise *only a few children ate their ice-cream* can be explained by a reason why a small number of children ate their ice-cream or a reason why a large number of children did not. In fact, given our knowledge of children and ice-cream, it is relatively difficult (in the time it takes to write a continuation) to think of plausible reasons for eating ice-cream that explain the small number. It is much easier to think of alternatives to ice-cream or properties of the ice-cream that might explain the large numbers who abstained.

Unlike a few, only a few seems to lead subjects to give explanations. The preferred explanation is in terms of the small number of whom the predicate is asserted. However, in some circumstances (like the ice-cream example), there are relatively more reasons for the relationship between the compset and the negation of the predicate that can equally explain the smallness of the number. In these cases only a few will be followed by an explanation in terms of the compset, hence bringing focus on the compset.

These arguments are the basis for supposing that there are two main triggers to compset reference. The first is explicit and implicit syntactic negativity. The second is the availability of the RWN inference pattern, which is plainly situation-dependent.

DISCUSSION: SOME RELATIONSHIPS BETWEEN COMPSET, NEGATIVITY, INFERENCE, AND MONOTONICITY

In this final section, we shall try to fit together some of the pieces. Our basic assumption is that compset focus is functionally useful. If something is true of a small number of X, then it is useful to have a class of expressions that causes the listener to ask the equivalent of : "What is it about the greater number of X making that something not true of them?" At the root of compset is the simple observation that quantifying expressions do not just have the function of specifying (however fuzzily) quantities: Many of them serve to draw attention to the quantities that they specify. Thus, not many has been treated as denying the "supposition" that many might have been the case (e.g. Clark, 1976). It effectively asserts that there is a deviation from expectation, and, as we have seen, deviations from expectation have the cognitive consequence of seeking an explanation of that deviation. Thus, compset focus emerges as a particular response to the need to give an explanation for a deviation signalled entirely by the quantifier itself. Compset focus also emerges from a more indirect route when the need for an explanation is triggered by other expressions that are not clearly negative, such as less than X and only a few.

Secondly, we propose that compset focusing is a processing pattern which de-emphasises the refset, so that at some point during processing it is effectively an empty set. This is not to say that if one asked a subject whether not many could mean none, he or she would reply affirmatively.

Rather, compset focus allows the possibility of an empty refset by taking attention away from it, and so makes tests for the allowance of the empty-set interpretation acceptable.

Thirdly, we suggest that the empty set is a configuration allowing those quantifiers that can produce it to appear intuitively mon dec, and therefore these expressions can be used to make statements that rely upon that property. The extent to which they are intuitively mon dec depends on other properties not standing in the way, as we illustrated earlier.[2] The acceptability of an item in a monotonicity test can therefore be seen as a soft constraint-satisfaction problem. In a case like *only a few*, which is dubious by all standards as mon dec, we have at least some evidence that compset focus does not *depend* on the quantifier being mon dec for this property. This is a principal part of our argument, of course.

The principal chain of argument is shown in Fig. 5.2. In summary, we suggest that clear negativity may trigger the compset focus pattern and RWN inference patterns. RWN inference patterns may also occur for other reasons, and lead to compset focus. Compset focusing as a process leads to the empty-set possibility, and this in turn makes some quantifiers seem to be mon dec. Of course this is speculative, and may turn out to be incorrect, but in the absence of any evidence to the contrary, we offer this formulation as a way of assembling some psychological data and some of the formal and linguistic properties of quantifiers.

In carrying out linguistic tests for negativity, such as tag tests and combination with negative polarity items, it quickly became clear that rather than acceptability being an all-or-none affair, it seemed to be gradeable. Because the categorisation of quantifiers as negative, mon dec, etc. depends on a yes or a no response, we have to ask whether quantifiers can be more-or-less negative, being fuzzy members of these categories, or whether the uncertainty comes from other sources. Our present view is that in some ways it is nonsensical to speak of something being more-or-less negative. Rather, any tests applied will be influenced by a variety of factors. On the other hand, we do suspect that certain categorisations that rely upon intuitions may admit to being a matter of degree. To illustrate some of the problems of categorisation, consider the case of *not quite all*.

This is an important quantifier for the compset focus argument, because it is taken as denoting a large amount. However, many people find this expression does not fit well in a test of the possibility of the empty set:

(14) Not quite all students went to the lecture, if any did.

It seems likely that this is because *not quite all* is so close to *all* in terms of the amount it denotes that the step to *none* is unreasonable in a direct assertion of the empty-set possibility. However, (14) is clearly better than (15), despite the fact that *a few* is nearer to *none* in terms of amount :

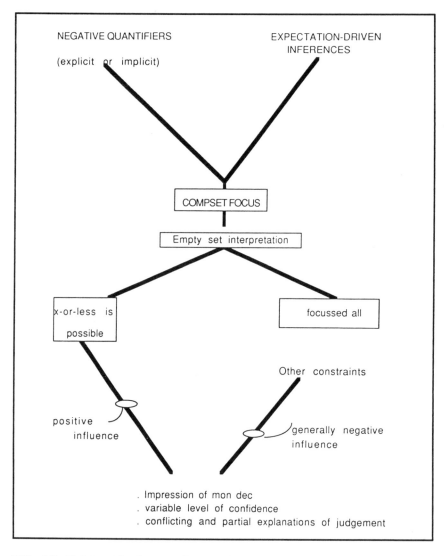

FIG. 5.2. Relationships between focus and other tests.

(15) A few of the students went to the lecture, if any did.[*]

We suggest that this is because *not quite all* allows the compset, whereas *a few* does not. It is magnitude of the gap that causes the problem in (14), which relies upon the explicit acceptance of the empty-set possibility. Testing for mon dec also yields an ill-fitting result:

(16) If not quite all of the students entered the race, then not quite all of the students entered the race early.

This seems to most people to be an invalid statement, and we suggest that this is because of the availability of the interpretation "just less than all", which effectively puts a limit on the free *less than X* interpretation. It is interference from the "just less than all" aspect that makes (16) seem invalid (and even unreasonable). Yet we can argue that the expression is in fact mon dec because it easily takes a negative polarity item in a declarative sentence (which necessarily means it is mon dec, according to Zwarts, 1991):

(17) Not quite all of the students study Shakespeare anymore.

In this case however, there is no need to evaluate explicitly the empty-set possibility of the *less than X* interpretation.

All of this means that the intuitive linguistic tests used in the analysis are influenced by the relation of what *not quite all* asserts relative to what supposition it generates. We suggest that it is used when *all* is to be expected, and that this is an important aspect of its condition of use, but that this very fact removes emphasis from the empty-set interpretation, so that the direct mon dec test fares badly. If we use the illogical use of *all* as an index of emphasis on the empty set, then our story is consistent. Thus (18) sounds reasonable (if strictly illogical), but (19) does not:

(18) Few of the fans went to the match. They all watched it on TV instead.

(19) Not quite all of the fans went to the match. They all watched it on TV instead.

The case of *not quite all* illustrates how the acceptability of test statements is not all or none. In the absence of a systematic scheme for understanding the relationships between various tests, and the several constraints that have an impact on acceptability, it seems to us that classification problems will not be easily solved. The present analysis is only a start, of course, and is quite speculative.

In the last two chapters we have shown that the quantifiers in quantified statements have an effect on the types of continuations that people produce. This is indicative of the different processing patterns that they set up. We have explored in some detail the notion of compset reference, and attempted to relate it to a variety of observations about quantifier semantics. A more systematic summary will be given in the final chapter.

Before that, in the next chapter, we shall explore some of the consequences of our observations, and extend some of the ways of differentiating among the uses of various expressions.

NOTES

1. Quantifiers in these formal treatments are defined as determiner + noun, for instance, *many cats* is a quantifier, whereas *many* is a determiner. We have called determiners quantifiers because this corresponds to the most common usage in psychology. But the distinction is important. It is determiner + noun that may be monotone in the present discussion. So, given *Many boys entered the race early*, it follows that *Many boys entered the race*. But if *Many decayed houses will be pulled down*, it does not follow that *Many houses will be pulled down*. It is the NOUNPHRASE which is monotonic, not the determiner. See Zwarts (1991) for further details

2. Defending their claim that all simple natural language quantifiers are monotone, Barwise and Cooper (1981) suggest that some quantifiers might give the illusion of being nonmonotone if that reading is blocked by conversational implicature. This is very similar to what we are arguing in claiming that in any linguistic test, both semantics and pragmatics will enter into the process of interpretation (and hence judgement).

CHAPTER SIX

Further Aspects of Inference

The focus and inference patterns discovered give quantifiers the capacity to influence reasoning and to enable other kinds of inferences that are important in communication. The three topics described later follow this line, and lead to further ways of constraining choice of quantifier in particular communication settings.

ATTRIBUTION

The study of attribution is a central topic in the cognitive approach to social phenomena (Hilton, 1988). It concerns the way in which people provide tentative explanations, reasons, or causes, for events or actions. Typically, for reasons of convenience, the events of interest are frequently depicted by written language descriptions, so that many findings in attribution theory are a function of the language used in the presentation of the vignettes (see Hilton, 1985, for a good discussion of this point). Consider the event *John kicks a dog*. Why should this happen? There are several possibilities (see e.g. Hilton, 1988; Hilton & Slugoski, 1986; Kelley, 1967), but among them are that there is something special about the dog (it may be prone to attack by passers-by), and something special about John (he may have a psychopathic attitude towards dogs). There are other possibilities, but for now these two will suffice. If one knew that *John often kicks dogs*, then one might suppose that John is a brute (something special about John). If, on the other hand, one knew that *almost everybody else took a kick at this particular dog*, then one would feel justified in asking what it was about the dog that brought about this disturbing behaviour. Notice that the attributional pattern is a function of what we can say or guess about baserates. In the present example, baserate information is provided in explicitly quantified form.

There are several ways in which quantifiers might play a role in triggering attributions. First of all, it might be argued that if John does something with a high frequency and other people do it with low frequency, then there is something of interest about John. The discrepancy in frequency alone may thus provide the basis for the attributions. On such a view, any means of signalling the difference should suffice, and thus quantifiers signalling similarly small proportions (such as *few* and *a few*) should have similar effects. Let us call this the *simple frequency signalling theory*. In contrast, we might suppose that it might not be enough to indicate just a small proportion, but that it must be indicated in a way that makes it clear that the proportion is *in itself* worthy of comment. Quantifiers and adverbs that we have seen to do this include *few* and *only a few*, *seldom* and *rarely*, but not *a few* and *occasionally*. This second view, that the quantifier must cue the unusualness of the small quantity it is denoting, we term the *focus control theory*, because the information provided by the quantifier is signalled through the way it influences inference. For instance, as we have seen, *only a few X do Y* seems to produce a mental state of querying *why so few X do Y*, whereas *few X do Y* signals the query *why so many X do not do Y*.

These two theories were examined in an empirical framework by Barton and Sanford (1990). An intuitive indication of how a combination of statement and background might control attribution is provided by the following :

(1) John listens to the local jazzband when it plays in town.
(2) Few others listen to the local jazzband when it plays in town.

It is our intuition on the basis of this pair that the frequency with which John does this (and the implicit quantification in (1) indicates that the action depicted is *generally the case*) is perceived as high relative to the explicitly signalled low frequency of others behaving in this way. The signalling is assumed to arise through the same mechanism, which leads us to question why this small number of others do not go. This in turn suggests that there is something special about John (he is tone-deaf, or seriously addicted to Jazz, for example). Such a pattern seems to stand in complete contrast to the following, which rather shows a bias towards there being something special about the band:

(3) John seldom listens to the local band.
(4) Few other people listen to the local band.

In both cases, the quantifiers signal a notably low frequency of appreciation of the band! Finally, although a quantifier might be thought of as denoting a low rather than a high frequency (*a few*), it appears that such quantifiers do not provide the attribution of an especially low rate:

(5) John listens to the local jazzband when it plays in town.
(6) A few other people listen to the local jazzband when it plays in town.

To test these intuitions, subjects were presented with a set of pairs of statements of the following form, where the brackets indicate options:

Mary [no quantifier] buys ice-cream from the local café.
[rarely]
[occasionally]
[only occasionally]

[no quantifier] other people buy ice-cream from the local café.
[a few]
[only a few]
[few]

Subjects were invited to indicate on a scale whether the sentences suggested (in this case) that there was something special about *Mary* or *the local cafe*. The alternative quantifiers and frequency adverbs give 16 different conditions, and 16 different scenarios were used. The results, shown in Fig. 6.1, show that there are differences between the pair *a few* and *occasionally*, and the other expressions. Thus, *occasionally* shows an attributional pattern that is relatively impervious to the quantifier with which it is paired. Similarly, *a few* is relatively impervious to the frequency adverb with which it is paired. Thus, *occasionally* and *a few* are not good for signalling abnormal conditions, whereas the other expressions in the study are. It is just those quantifiers and frequency adverbs that lead to reason-continuations that have the effect of forcing attributional patterns one way or the other.

Note, however, that even the weak compset-licensing expression only a few and its counterpart only occasionally are just as good at controlling attributions as the stronger compset licencers. This suggests that although it is expressions inducing focus on reasons that influence the perception of

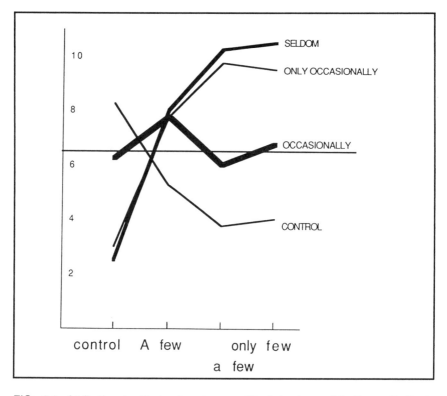

FIG. 6.1. Attributional effects due to quantifier/adverb combinations. Ordinate indicates the attribution pattern for a given combination. Zero = extreme subject abnormality (something unusual about the subject), 13 = extreme object abnormality. (From Barton & Sanford, 1990, with permission.)

abnormality, and hence attribution, it is possibly not compset focus that is critical here, but rather the capacity to induce reason-focusing behaviour in general.

A second point worth noting is a possible interpretation of how implicitly and explicitly quantified statements might be represented and compared. We noted in Chapters 1 and 2 that generalisations such as "John visits the cinema when he is in town" and "Other people visit the cinema when they are in town" are not to be understood as universal statements. Indeed, the first statement might be equated with "John often ..." and the latter with "Many other people visit the cinema occasionally when they are in town". Thus, there is an inherent problem with the simple frequency-signalling point of view anyway: There is no clear way to determine which frequencies are to be compared. Rather, the contrasts elicited by the use of reason-focusing quantifiers must be due to inference control alone.

EXPECTATIONS AND HIGHER-ORDER INTERPRETATIONS

The focus-control property also introduces the possibility that when certain quantifiers are used by a speaker, listeners may be able to infer something about the kinds of beliefs the speaker has about the situation that is being described. For instance, suppose that a speaker says: *not many students went to the party*. This should make the listener wonder why the majority did not go. But suppose instead that the question is whether the speaker of the utterance had expected more to be there, a priori? Does his use of *not many* indicate that more were to be expected? Such a view is certainly in line with the idea that *not many* denies a "supposition" that many (or more than not many) might have been the case (Clark, 1976). Thus, one might expect the listener to presume that the speaker would have expected more than was in fact the case, or at least have been surprised at the small number, even if his prior expectation was not an active one. Similar arguments can be made for all of the other marked quantifiers discussed earlier. The possibility that quantifiers serving to comment on the small proportions they denote imply that the speaker had higher a priori expectations was examined by Moxey and Sanford (1993), following Moxey (1986).

We shall call interpretations of the prior expectations of speakers and listeners *higher-order interpretations*. These interpretations form an effectively infinite set, as they correspond to mutual knowledge states. We shall restrict ourselves here to the two levels that have been investigated, and which may be understood by looking at Fig. 6.2. This depicts a simple situation in which Fiona is reporting to Iain a fact about children who went to a party. Moxey (1986; Moxey & Sanford, 1993) conjectured that Fiona's utterance may be interpreted at a number of levels. Level 1 corresponds to the simple interpretation of amount being denoted. If required, Iain should be able to assign a numerical value at that level, along the lines discussed in Chapter 2. But in her utterance, Fiona may be providing information at other levels. Level 2, for instance, represents the impression the listener (Iain) might have of the speaker's (Fiona's) prior expectations regarding the proportion of children who went to the party. Level 3 corresponds to the listener's (Iain's) impression of what the speaker (Fiona) thought the listener (Iain) might have expected before the fact. In each instance, a subject might be requested to provide percentages or other numerical values for levels 2 and 3 in just the same way as they were for level 1.

These questions are clearly meaningful in some contexts. For example, a speaker may explicitly provide the same information:

(7) I was surprised that many of the children went to Julie's party.
(8) You'd be surprised to know that many of the children went to Julie's party.

FIG. 6.2. Showing the three levels of interpretation discussed in the present chapter.

Of course, the question at hand is whether such information can be gleaned from a single quantified statement. We have argued that there are reasons to suppose that some higher-order interpretation should be possible on the basis of quantifier, but have provided no grounds for differentiating between levels 2 and 3. Clearly, levels 2 and 3 are conceptually different, yet there is no obvious a priori way of making independent predictions about them. Moxey and Sanford (1993), however, found that they appear to be empirically distinguishable.

In order to investigate expectations directly, Moxey and Sanford used the three scenarios used for the level 1 study described earlier (pp. 31–33). These scenarios had different baserate expectations: low (survey, 27%), medium (party conference, 50%) and high (residents association, 66%). These values, it will be recalled, were obtained by asking subjects what they would expect in each scenario. Now, one might suppose that if people come from the same social and linguistic community, they would all have broadly similar ideas about baseline default values such as these. So if we ask one member of the community what another might be believed to expect, the response should be similar to his own unless there are grounds to suppose some different expectation. Furthermore, a listener would assume a speaker to assume that a listener has similar expectations, an assumption of mutual knowledge (c.f. Clark & Marshall, 1981; Perner & Garnham, 1989). Accordingly, one might anticipate answers to level 2 and level 3 questions (Fig. 6.2) that are about the same as baserate estimates if the quantifiers themselves contribute no information about expectations at levels 2 and 3. And even if quantifiers do contribute such information, we would anticipate judgements to be related to baseline.

An experiment was carried out in which the 3 scenarios were combined with 10 quantifiers to produce 30 materials. Two possible questions could be asked. At level 2 the question was what percentage the subjects thought the *writer* must have expected before the facts. At level 3, the question was what percentage the subjects thought the writer believed they (the *subjects or readers*) had expected before the facts. The materials combined with the questions resulted in 60 conditions. A large number of subjects was tested: No subject made more than one judgement. The design was thus entirely independent-groups to eliminate transfer and contrast effects.

At level 2 the results show a clear effect of prior expectation on the judgements produced, and a significant variation of estimates for quantifiers. The results are shown in Fig. 6.3(a). There is a clear effect of baserate on the estimates provided, but there are also reliable differences in the interpretations given to different quantifiers, so quantifiers are having an effect. Because there was only a very weak interaction between these two main factors, and because of the complexity of the data, we shall consider the data collapsed over scenarios, as shown in Fig. 6.3(b). This is the most powerful way of looking at the data, and also the clearest in these early explorations. The estimates generated by only two of the quantifiers presented show systematic reliable differences to those of the other quantifiers: *a few*, and *quite a few*. Both of these produce estimates that are reliably lower than the other quantifiers; the precise pattern of reliable differences is indicated in Fig. 6.3(b).

The effect with *a few* is consistent with our earlier arguments, and was interpreted as follows. If a speaker (writer) simply states that *a few of the X did Y*, then he is singling out a small proportion, but is not inviting any sort of comment on the small proportion through the quantifier. A listener (reader) should infer that the speaker was not surprised by the small proportion, and thus that his prior expectations were not violated. In short, if anything, the listener should infer that the speaker expected a low proportion. On the other hand, if a low-ranking quantifier is used that induces inferences about the small number (*few, only a few, not many*, etc.), then the inference should be that the speaker did find the number worthy of comment, from which it follows that his expectations were violated, which is consistent with the level 2 interpretation that the speaker had expected a higher number. If this reasoning is correct, then it accounts for the pattern of results with *a few*: This quantifier produced reliably lower estimates than the other low-ranking expressions.

There is no reason to suppose that the high-ranking expressions *many*, *a lot*, and *very many* convey any element of comment on the high proportions they denote, and therefore level 2 estimates of these should also be high, which they are. However, an interesting case arises with the expression *quite a few*. This produced low estimates too. There has been no independent analysis of the properties of *quite a few*[1], unfortunately, so we have no independent means of knowing what focusing properties this might have (although all intuitive tests show it to be refset focusing). In the interim, we simply rephrase the results and claim that *quite a few* may denote a moderate proportion X%, but imply that less than X% was expected.

At level 3, many of the level 2 phenomena replicate, but the situation is more complicated. Figure 6.4(a) shows the effect of baseline expectation on estimates. This effect was reliable, along with a main effect of quantifier, but there was no interaction between the two. The quantifier effect is shown pooled over scenarios in Fig. 6.4(b). There are more reliable differences in these level 3 estimates than at level 2.

First, the results found with *a few* and *quite a few* replicate: These produce low estimates of prior expectation. This gives us more faith in the finding at level 2 with *quite a few*, which was unexpected. Accordingly, we suggest that a description of *quite a few* is as follows: *Assert X%, and suppose that less than X% should have been the case*.

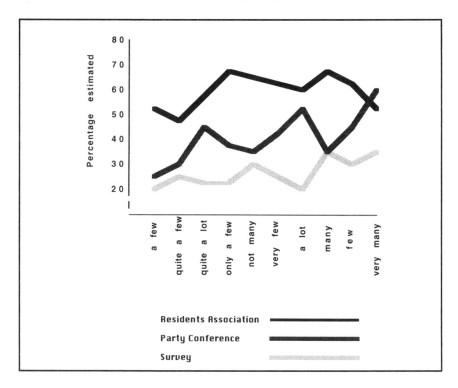

FIG. 6.3(a). Mean value of percentage interpretation for level 2. Lines are for clarity; quantifiers are ordered by mean ascending values. (From Moxey & Sanford, 1993, with permission.)

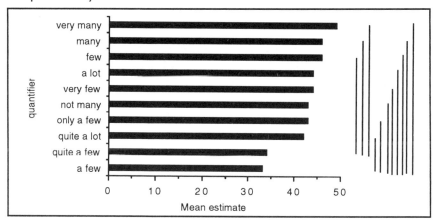

FIG. 6.3(b). Mean values for level 2 interpretation when data are collapsed over scenarios. The bar lines denote pairs which differ reliably from each other at the 5% level or better. (From Moxey & Sanford, 1993, with permission.)

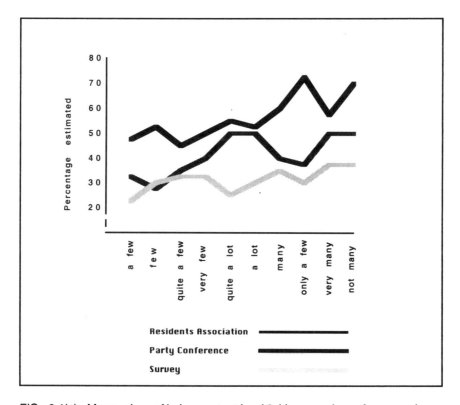

FIG. 6.4(a). Mean values of judgements at level 3. Lines are drawn for convenience of illustration. Quantifiers are ordered in terms of ascending mean values.

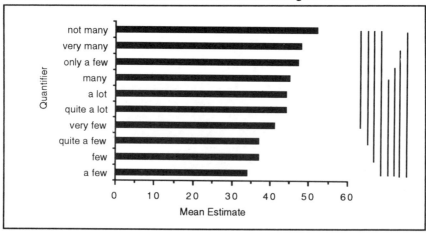

FIG. 6.4(b). Mean values of estimates at level 3 when data are collapsed over scenarios. Bars indicate which are reliable at the 5% level or better.

The biggest surprise is the separation of *few* and *not many* at this level. *Not many* produces the highest estimates, and *few* produces the second lowest, not being differentiated from *a few*. Because of the pattern of reliable differences, there is no reason at all to suppose that this difference is spurious. Taken at face value, the results suggest the following: When a speaker uses the term *few*, the inference that the speaker believed the listener to have expected more is not drawn. In contrast, when the expression *not many* is used, the inference that the speaker believed the listener to have expected more *is* drawn. So there appears to be a difference between these two terms as a function of level of interpretation. If this is indeed the case, then the difference should have consequences for communication. This is demonstrated in the next section.

As a final comment about higher-order interpretations, we should make it clear that such effects as we have obtained here are forced in that we specifically requested subjects to make an explicit judgement. While this procedure has at least demonstrated that subjects *can* make the inferences underlying such judgements, this does not mean that they always *do*. In fact, it seems very likely that such inferences will only be drawn when they are of interest to the listener. For example, higher-order aspects of communication like these may be more crucial to those having a love affair than to those having little real interest in each others opinions. Of course, this is a general issue going beyond mere quantifiers. Returning to the data at hand, it is also possible that the use of higher-level interpretations is a function of both education (our subjects were all university students) and of task demands.

CHOICE OF QUANTIFIER IN VIGNETTES

In communication settings, we would expect any or all of the observed features that differentiate quantifiers to play a role. Thus, in the setting of an attribution study, the capacity of a quantifier to instigate a search for reasons seems to be enough for it to influence attributional patterns. Other situations might draw on even finer distinctions. Recently we have been experimenting with the vignette methodology in order to illustrate this and also add to the kinds of distinctions already discovered. The essence of the vignette methodology is to create a description of a situation, ending with the need for one of two protagonists to speak. The subject is then given a choice of things that the speaker might say, and is invited to choose the best of these, or to rank-order them, or otherwise indicate relative acceptability. We first investigated the *car salesman scenario,* and we believe its explanation to rely on several of the distinctions we have made.

Imagine a situation in which a car salesman has been discussing with a client possible cars to be purchased. The client has asked about a number of cars, but keeps coming back to the same one. He asks about the reliability of the model, which is not known to him. The salesman replies "Well, put it this way, few of these cars need more than a basic service within the first three years". The customer is (one hopes) impressed. But if the salesman had said "A few of these cars need more than a basic service within the first three years", the effect would be to put the customer off the model. There are several explanations for this, but they all relate to focusing properties. In order to examine whether acceptable answers are restricted to quantifiers with compset-focusing properties, Sanford et al. (in prep.) invited subjects to either rank-order the acceptability of answers the salesperson might give, or give a simple acceptability rating on a scale ranging from "completely acceptable" to "totally unacceptable", thus providing two ways of looking at preferences. The quantifiers used in the main study were *few, not many, only a few,* and *a few.*

Regardless of the task, the results were the same. The order of preference was first for *few*. After this came *only a few* and *not many* (whose order was basically undifferentiated), with *a few* firmly at the bottom of the list. The result suggests that refset focusing is undesirable in this context, with *only a few* falling short of *few* in the preference ranks. In a subsidiary condition, in which a very low percentage (5%) was substituted for *a few*, the ranking of the percentage was low, although 5% is in fact a low failure rate. Focus is clearly playing a role here; mere percentages are not enough.

However, although compset focusers are preferred, there is a complication: *not many*, a strong compset focuser, has a low preference and absolute rating, almost as low as *only a few*, and in any case reliably lower than *few*, yet *few* and *not many* are often treated as essentially (though not strictly) equivalent. The only other situation where a very clear difference between *not many* and *few* has been found was in the comparisons of expectations given at levels 2 and 3 in the preceding section. Our current view is that in using *not many*, the speaker is allowing the inference that the speaker expects the listener to have expected *many* to be the case, and that this is something that it is desirable to keep out of the mind of the listener. *Few* does not do this.

In a subsequent study, we attempted to set up a situation where implying a high level of expectation at level 3 would be desirable. If this could be done, then we would predict that *not many* would be preferred to *few* as a response. To this end we constructed the following scenario:

Imagine an old man who takes a great interest in the local amateur football team, and who is extremely concerned about the falling numbers of fans who attend. Last Saturday he had to miss the game because he was ill in bed. His friend went instead, and reported back later that day. The old man was keen to know how many fans had attended. In reality, none of the fans had turned up. His friend had to tell him this, but hedged, saying something like: "[Quantifier] of the fans went to the match. Well, in fact, none did."

The task was to choose the most appropriate quantifier from *hardly any, not many, few, only a few*, and *a few*. *Not many* was considered to be more appropriate than *few* in this case. We would argue at present that this is because *not many* leads to an inference in which the speaker engages his expectations. In contrast, *few* does not. So, although both *not many* and *few* only implicate that *not-none* is the case (this being defeasible), and both admit *none* as a possible interpretation with equal ease, in the vignette setting there is a preference. We suspect that this is due to the difference of expectations.

Obviously this is all very tentative, and there is much more to do in refining the vignette methodology, but it does appear promising. In less subtle circumstances quite predictable effects can be obtained. Thus, if conditions exist where it is desirable for the speaker to induce compset focus, then of course the opposite should hold. Focus on the refset should occur when the speaker wants the listener to concentrate on the set of things for which the predicate is true, even if it is very small. Such an example occurs when a doctor has to advise a patient of there being a very low (but finite) probability of surviving an operation. Sanford et al. (in prep) tested this idea, and found that the rank-ordering changed dramatically, with *a few* and *only a few* being preferred over *few, not many*, and lastly *hardly any* as quantifiers describing the number of survivors. We ascribe this pattern to the exclusion of null-set interpretations for the preferred quantifiers (but more weakly in the case of *only few*, of course), which removes precisely the possibility that the patient does not want to hear!

CONCLUDING REMARKS

That quantifiers only trigger attributional patterns if they induce reason-seeking behaviour is a simple point, but it is gratifying that things are at least that predictable. Reason-seeking is assumed to be due to an expression denying or otherwise bringing into question a supposition in Clark's (1976) sense. When things are brought into question, the cognitive result is to ask why. We have suggested that the form of the cognitive "why?" is focused on either compset or refset, depending on the expression in question. However, the notion of supposition needs refinement, and we have asked whose suppositions (we called them expectations) are violated.

The higher-order interpretation task was designed to see whether expectations are brought into question by some quantifiers but not by others (they are, as our discussion up to now would predict). But the expectations signalled by quantifiers fractionate between level 2 and level

3 interpretations, a finding that we believe could not really have been foreseen. In particular, *not many* and *few* clearly separate. The vignette tasks were designed to provide a means of looking at preference patterns in specific communication settings. Clearly, the task needs a good deal of refinement, but seems promising in that it separates out situations that require compset and refset focusing expressions (the hospital patient), and those that require the speaker to engage tacitly the listener's expectations (the football match), or explicitly ignore them (the car salesman).

From the point of view of differentiating quantifiers, with this batch of findings we show that *few* and *not many* differentiate where they did not before, and that *quite a few* seems to suggest that more than was expected turned out to be the case. We might speculate that *quite a lot* works the other way, the supposition at levels 2 and 3 being that more were expected than was the case. This is not inconsistent with the data obtained, but obviously a specific test should be carried out. However, different functions of this sort would make sense, because *quite a few* and *quite a lot* produce very similar level 1 interpretations (Moxey & Sanford, 1993), and sometimes indistinguishable interpretations (McDonald, 1990).

NOTE

1.   *Quite* has been treated within the scaling framework as a multiplier of the scale value of basic expressions like *a lot* and *a few* (e.g. Cliff, 1957). In Moxey and Sanford (1993), when it is treated this way, it appeared to make the values of the expressions it modified less extreme. However, *quite* may also be used in the sense of precisely (as in *not quite all → not as much* as *exactly all*). In some ideolects, this use appears to predominate. To our knowledge, no study has treated *quite* as a way of directly indicating a deviation from expectation, along the lines of Wierzbicka's (1986) approximatives.

CHAPTER SEVEN

Towards a Psychological Account of Nonlogical Quantifiers

This chapter completes our review of existing psychologically oriented work on nonlogical quantifiers, and its relation to other approaches. One of our tasks was to try to explain the large variety of quantifiers that exist in natural language. The bulk of the book was then concerned with exploring how different quantifiers influence the processing patterns that follow in the wake of encountering quantified statements. In the first section of this final chapter this work is summarised, and we speculate about some further differentiations that might be possible. In the second section we summarise some aspects of quantifier meaning, from a psychological perspective, and consider how other expressions might be treated in a similar way. Finally, we discuss how the work might be incorporated into a more general account of text comprehension.

OVERVIEW: DIFFERENTIATION AND USAGE

Comment-generators versus Amounts

When a speaker chooses a particular quantifier, it will usually be chosen in preference to other expressions. What is it that differentiates one quantifier from another? The bulk of this book has been concerned with that question. Quantifiers surely cannot be differentiated in terms of the numbers or proportions they denote, a point laboured in Chapters 2 and 3 and reinforced further in this one, although they obviously can be ranked with respect to one another up to a point. The solution to their differentiation, we suggested, lies in the patterns of inferential activity they trigger.

In the face of a quantified utterance like *[Quantifier] of the A do B*, which means that some proportion P of A do B, attention might be drawn to:

(a) *Simple action continuation*: What the P did next, etc.
(b) *Consequence of an amount*: The effect of the amount P doing B
(c) *Reason why*: The reason why P do B
(d) *Reason why not*: The reason why the remainder (1–P), do not do B

These are the principal forms of continuation we identified in the continuation studies, and we believe that they constitute meaningful, interpretable patterns. Furthermore, we hypothesise that the variety of expressions has been developed partly to allow just these basic kinds of inference pattern to be invited in the listener by the use of relatively simple language.

Assertions of Amount

Quantifiers that normally lead to continuations of type (a) place attention on what P did next (or some other simple continuation) without any aspect of the largeness or smallness of P being incorporated into processing, unless some expectation is violated. Our suggestion is that such quantifiers simply assert that there is some number or amount, which may be small (e.g. *a few*) or large (e.g. *many*), where the meaning of large or small is situationally determined. All expressions in this category are positive: *a few, some?, many, most?, X%*. The question marks indicate that we do not have any direct psychological evidence to support our claim that these expressions simply reflect an amount assertion. Finer differentiations of amount through modifiers such as *very* and *quite*, we suggest, are mostly to do with modifying the strength of the assertion, rather than the amount *per se* (although, when subjects are required to assign amounts to expressions, differences may appear). These quantifiers may also convey information about monotonicity (they may be monotone increasing).

Failures to signal comments depend on expectations not being violated. This is important, as a violation of expectation has the cognitive impact of causing the listener to seek reasons. In many situations, a listener may have no strong expectations at all. For instance, one might not have any prior expectations about whether an unspecified set of students would enjoy a lecture on some unspecified topic. So, whether one heard that *A few* or that *Many of the students enjoyed the lecture*, one is unlikely to seek or expect an explanation relating to the proportion of students. If, on the other hand, the quantifier mismatched expectation, then reasons would be expected. The utterance *Many children hated Santa Claus* falls into this class, inviting reasons why this should be the case, such as that he smelled of whisky (i.e. is not the "real" Santa Claus). However, the reasons, when they occur, will be of type (d) listed earlier.

Such an expectation violation relies upon mapping the utterance onto normative background knowledge. Because it is normal to like Santa, it has to be inferred that there is something special about Santa. But noncomment-generating quantifiers will not create a search for explanations unless there is a violation of some presumed norm. This explains their failure to influence attribution patterns when there is no obvious violation of expectation (see Chapter 6).

A final remark about the idea that quantifiers denote numbers, or distributions of numbers, is in order. If, as Barwise and Cooper (1981) claim, all simple natural language quantifiers are either mon inc or mon dec, then they cannot denote simple amounts (such as X%), or even amounts with variance (such as X% plus or minus Y%). Natural language equivalents of these, such as *about X%* and *roughly Z%*, that is numbers modified by approximatives, are not monotone (and therefore for Barwise and Cooper, reasonably, are not simple quantifiers). With respect to monotone quantifiers (such as *few* and *many*), this observation would automatically rule out most versions of the unidimensional hypothesis discussed in Chapters 1 and 2, because they are founded on the view that such translations are possible. So, it is fruitless to try to devise a dictionary of such mappings either as an explanation of human usage, or as the basis for a computational system for dealing with quantified information, for instance in an expert system.

Of course, even if quantifiers are formulated as *X or less* or *X or more*, there remains the question of what determines X, and there will still be room to express preferences for regions of the intervals [0 – X] or [X – all], if necessary. This makes monotonicity a complication for scale-mapping, and it is still necessary to determine how to specify X, preferences over the interval, and so on.[1] Once again, let us raise the alternative: When someone uses a quantifier, it only roughly specifies "large amount relative to some criterion" or "small amount relative to some criterion"; its focusing properties may then indicate monotonicity. If this is the case, then the actual computation of what is the value of X, should it be demanded in a task, will depend on the situation in question, and what is the critical criterion (or criteria) under consideration. There is no need for X to be part of the semantics of the expression concerned; it is a matter of problem solving.

Compset and Refset Focusers

When a quantified statement is made and does not violate a quantitative expectation, and yet generates a continuation falling into patterns (b) – (d), then the quantifier is a comment generator in its own right. The most typical examples of such quantifiers are negatives, but they are not necessarily negative. For instance, *more than X do Y* is not negative, yet it directs attention to reasons why *more than X do Y* is being asserted (that is, a category (c) response).

The last two classes of inference are most commonly elicited by the comment-generating group in our studies. The last class in the list, RWN, is associated with the compset focus pattern. We suggested that the compset pattern may be brought about in two ways: By being directly associated with negatives (that is, learned as a salient question to ask about situations in which negatives arise), and also by RWN being the most readily available information that comes to mind. We suggested that explicit negatives (*not many*) and, later in development, implicit negatives (*few*) come to signal compset patterns of focus directly, because those are the kinds of contexts in which they are learned. With *only a few*, on the other hand, compset focus comes about primarily through the kinds of explanations which are available in the circumstances. Either way, compset and RWN is a way of explaining why the predicate is not true of a quantified assertion, and as such is plainly a concomitant of the idea of a supposition suggested by Clark (1976): If at one and the same time *not many did X* (a small number or proportion) is asserted, yet at some level *many* is supposed as a possibility (as appears to be the case with *not many*), then the system should be focused on the discrepancy, effectively asking "why did so many not do X?", with answers being found in the domain of RWN. Thus, the idea of denial of a supposition may be the generator of the system seeking RWN, leading to focus on the compset.

Higher-order Interpretation Patterns

If compset configurations come about because a supposition has been violated, then the question of who holds the belief that constitutes the supposition may be asked. To our knowledge, the only work that has directly addressed this issue empirically is our own, as outlined in the preceding chapter. In general, we found that listeners believed that speakers themselves held the beliefs corresponding to suppositions (which themselves may be the result of default norms). Listeners also believed that the speaker thought that they, the listeners, would hold those same beliefs. Although this evidence is indirect, the pattern of results from the higher-order expectation task is at least consistent with such a view. Most of the negatives conformed to this pattern, but the term *few* did not. On the contrary, judgements about this expression suggested that although a listener might expect a producer to use it if the *speaker* might have expected more, the listener did not assume the speaker to believe that he, the listener, expected more. This pattern was used to explain some of the vignette judgements in Chapter 6. Although we have not explored the generality of the effect, we would hope that similar differentiations might be seen with other explicit / implicit negatives, such as *short/not tall*, *forbid/not allow*, etc. In fact, results from the *forbid/not allow* distinction, investigated in the context of questionnaire design (Hippler & Schwarz, 1986), show that statements containing the word *forbid* are considered to be stronger than those containing the expression *not allow*, so that when questions are framed using these expressions, which one is used influences the responses given by people who do not hold strong prior opinions. Conceivably, this is because *forbid* does not signal to the listener that the speaker is taking the listener's prior beliefs into account. Although this is admittedly speculative, it seems to be a reasonable hypothesis for further investigation, and may provide an explanation why *forbid* (like *few*) sounds formal and aloof compared with *not allow* (and *not many*).

Our studies of interpretations at levels 2 and 3 revealed another interesting effect. The expression *quite a few* seemed to be interpreted as something like, *Someone (speaker, listener) might suppose: Expect a few. But there turned out to be more.* As yet, there is no other data on this question, from continuation studies, for example. If the analysis is correct, then the processor should be trying to explain the discrepancy, and therefore we would expect subjects presented with statements headed with *quite a few* to provide reasons for the greater number than was expected. This remains to be established. Another question concerns the comparable expression *quite a lot*. Although this means less than *a lot*, it may, by analogy with *quite a few,* mean that a lot was expected but in fact less turned out to be the case. This suggestion is consistent with the data. If the view is correct, then we might expect continuations to be about why *a little less than a lot* was the case. Such data are not available.

Other Differentiations: Mass and Count

We have dealt almost exclusively with count expressions, and it is at least believable that the same arguments would apply to mass quantifiers (*a bit, a little, a dod, a drop, a lot, much, very much*). Some parallels are obvious. For instance, the *little/a little* distinction corresponds to the *few/a few* distinction (it is easy to show a parallel in terms of the linguistic tests that are used to check monotonicity). Perhaps *not much* and *little* parallel *not many/few*. Apart from these observations, mass versus count raises another interesting problem. Mass expressions may sometimes be used with respect to count situations, but not vice-versa (see McCawley, 1981, for a logico-linguistic discussion). So, we can speak of *a lot of the students* or *many of the students* and the result sounds almost synonymous. Is there anything at all that governs our choice of *many* versus *a lot*? One possible approach might deserve future consideration. Perhaps *a lot* is used for countable entities when it is desirable to treat the large number as an undifferentiated mass, whereas *many* is used when the fact that the group is composed of individuals is to be made more accessible. Thus, for instance, there may be a slight preference for choosing to say *many students attended the rally* when it is important that people realise that the students attended for a variety of different, personal reasons, but *a lot* would be used to turn attention away from differentiation towards just the large number. Such an argument is about connotation rather than denotation, of course, and relies on the subtle weak use of a semantic constraint applicable in one domain in another. The whole issue is ripe for future investigation.

THE MEANING OF QUANTIFIERS AND RELATED TERMS
General Comments

The material surveyed in this book suggests that if we wish to specify how a quantifier is used, and how it is interpreted, then the answer does not lie in scale-mappings or membership functions on the one hand, nor in the specification of simple states of the world (numbers, proportions, minimum numbers, maximum numbers, etc.) on the other. To the extent that quantifiers are associated with numbers, we believe that represented (learned) associations of this type will be limited, and that, typically, a request for numbers or proportions will in effect be a request for the listener to do some problem solving. When subjects are required to put numbers to quantifiers in simple situations such as those discussed in Chapter 2, there are developmental trends in the consistency with which numbers are assigned to quantifiers, and there is a developmental trend in that quantifiers become slightly more differentiated, but the differentiation is limited, as already indicated (Pollard, Service, & Hunter, 1992). We suggest that an association between a quantifier and an amount (expressed as number or proportion) is very much a secondary characteristic, and to make such a mapping explicitly will often involve quite complex problem-solving. For instance, not only is situational baserate a factor, but interpretations may indeed vary with the perceived intention of the speaker. Certainly no really acid test has ever been carried out. Even if evidence for interpretation onto a scale did occur, it seems inevitable that a search for truth conditions expressed in such terms will at best be situation-specific and fuzzy.

In contrast to such an approach, our suggestion is that quantifiers are *mental operators*: They exert an influence on the patterns of inference that follow in the wake of utterances containing them; that is, they are controllers of what is attended to. We suggest further that their development in a language is to make available the simple means for directing patterns of thought and reasoning about quantities rather than to enable a numerical or strict logical (truth-functional) interpretation. Therefore, in selecting a quantifier for use, the user will make a selection that accords with these inference patterns when it is important to do so, and failure to do so will mean that the quantifier selected is a suboptimal choice.

We believe our conclusions regarding the meaning of quantifiers are in many ways compatible with the suggestions of Barwise and Cooper (1981) in that they concentrate upon specifying how natural language expressions fit into the Generalised Quantifier Theory, which is about the kinds of inferences licensed by expressions, rather than being about the (numerical) values that may be associated with expressions. If a particular natural language expression (quantifier) denotes a state of affairs that corresponds to some category within the theory, then it is possible to say what inferences it licenses: That is, what necessarily true things follow if the quantified assertion is true. For instance, if a quantifier is monotone, then a particular (formal, deductive) pattern of inference is licensed. The same applies to other properties Barwise and Cooper investigated. These logical properties stand regardless of the fact that the numbers or proportions of individuals denoted by a quantifier are not addressed. As we saw in Chapter 5, all of this depends on natural language quantifiers fitting linguistic tests that correspond to properties of the theory, and this fit may not be perfect (especially in the important case of mon dec expressions). We therefore believe that when an expression that is not deductively mon dec is used as though it were, it is being interpreted as though it were a true mon dec quantifier.

We have made some efforts here to link aspects of logico-linguistic analyses to psychology. If the semantic analysis of natural language quantifiers relies on the intuitive acceptability of linguistic tests, or on (analytically) insupportable acts of inference, then there is a need to explain where those intuitions come from, and how they correspond to *reliable* uses of quantifiers. For instance, if under a given circumstance speakers and listeners make common assumptions about monotonicity, then it is pragmatically reliable, even if it not formally necessary. How the acceptance that a particular property is intended in a given situation comes about is a central link between natural language semantics and formal semantics.

Our view is that possible interpretations are under the control of soft constraints, so that the extent to which some possible interpretation is paramount will depend on the current situational context. This in turn means that whether or not a particular (formal) inference pattern is perceived as being licensed will correspondingly depend on the current situational context. Such considerations provide a very direct way of linking psychological theories of processes with the ideal of providing a logical description of quantifiers. Our suggestions in these few chapters are very much preliminary attempts in that direction: Indeed, this way of framing the problem is not that obvious. It may be the case that such a formulation has not motivated much research to date because psychologists have concentrated almost exclusively on *all*, *some*, *no (one)* and *not all*, which are easily understood as having obvious logical properties. (We should point out though that the extent to which pragmatics colours the interpretations naturally given to these expressions is an indication that the fit of natural language to logic, even here, is far from perfect).

Learning and Meaning

We have scarcely touched on the question of how quantifiers are learned, yet this is plainly a central issue in developing an adequate psychological account. As we saw, the data of Pollard et al. (1992) appeared to show that children gradually learn to assign different numbers to high-ranking and low-ranking quantifiers. But how could children come to associate numbers (or proportions) with quantifiers? They would have to encounter quantifiers used as descriptions in situations where an amount (number or proportion) was clearly presented, and this would have to happen enough times for a reasonably reliable probability distribution to be built up if the mapping were to be much use in communication. Relatively simple associative machinery, like feed-forward neural nets, can easily learn to map numbers onto expressions, because they can easily and quickly form representations of probability-density functions (Doing, 1991). There is a problem, however. Just how many situations are actually encountered in which numerical information is actually known? Obviously, in many settings where quantified statements are encountered, there will be no independent co-occurring numerical or proportion input. To the authors' knowledge, there are no empirical data on this important issue at present. If difficulties might be foreseen for the appropriate acquisition conditions holding for learning distributions, what about for the conditions for learning relative orderings in terms of *strength of assertion* (as discussed in Chapter 3)? Here the problem is much less difficult: Provided the ordering of basic expressions such as *none, a few, many, all* are learned, most of the differences from then on occur through the medium of modifiers (*very, quite*, and so on). Presumably the use of modifiers like these is learned in the many contexts in which they occur, most of which will have little to do with quantification, but rather serve an intensifying or hedging function. (It is interesting that such adverbs have been treated as multipliers of the supposed scale values of expressions on which they operate [Cliff, 1957; Zadeh, 1975; see also Lakoff, 1972, and McCawley, 1981, for a discussion]). Our own work suggested that *very* may amplify the force of an utterance in general, whereas *quite* seems to have implications for interpretation at levels above 1 (the simple), as well as at level 1 itself. A little later we shall see how approximatives that are related terms have now been given an analysis beyond those tied to scales, and more closely resembling our analysis of quantifiers.

The need for investigations of the circumstances in which early exposure to quantified statements takes place is a general one. Our claim that quantifiers have attention-controlling functions clearly demands an exploration in terms of acquisition. But here it seems more plausible that the necessary ingredients for easy learning of attention-control patterns would be present in situations where quantifiers are used than it is plausible that numerical information would be present. In a preliminary search of some naturally occurring examples of *few* and *not many* in use, we have noted that they frequently appear in contexts where reasons-why-not are being given, thus providing the ingredients for learning just such usage. Although examples of (pronominal) compset reference *per se* are rare in spontaneous text, we have already suggested that such a referential effect may be secondary, as the individuals in a set only have significance because of the things they are mapped onto. Thus compset entities only have significance, a *raison d'être*, because they are mapped onto inferential structures supporting RWN inference patterns. We therefore suggest that learning the inference (focus) patterns associated with particular expressions is probably a lot easier than learning number-mappings ever could be. It is obvious that a programme of research into acquisition would provide data capable of deciding between some of the views put forward in this book. We have in mind not just the scale-mapping issue, but also such questions as whether the ability to make a judgement of (say) decreasing monotonicity depends on prior acquisition of the compset-licensing property.

Other Quantity Expressions

There is little reason to doubt that analyses similar to those applied to quantifiers could be applied to other expressions. At various times we have touched on possible correspondences between frequency adverbs and quantifiers. Thus *seldom* seems to bear a strong relation to *few*, *not quite always* to *not quite all, often* to *many, occasionally* to *a few*, and so on. We have a little evidence that focus patterns (in terms of inference type) of these pairs correspond (Moxey et al., 1990), and that similar parallels occur with the attribution paradigm (Chapter 6: Barton & Sanford, 1990). Furthermore, Ladusaw (1979) showed that some of these adverbs will take negative polarity items in simple declarative sentences. Thus frequency adverbs seem to be likely candidates for a parallel to quantifiers, and because they are just as common as quantifiers in questionnaire work (or more so), an investigation of such a possibility is well-motivated.

One important class of quantifiers to which we have not paid much attention is simple numbers, such as *10%* or *1.231,* and numbers modified by approximatives, such as *roughly 60*. There are two obvious and important points to be made about these. The first concerns the mapping of approximatives onto scales. Clearly, *roughly, vaguely, about*, and so on signal that there is an acceptable range around the value being modified. As with quantifiers, however, the range being specified is complex and situation-dependent. For example, about 20 might mean 20 plus or minus 5. On the other hand, about 23 does not mean between 17 and 28. It appears that "round" numbers admit to larger approximative boundaries than do other numbers. In a recent study in our laboratory, Judith Ramsay (unpublished data) found this to be the case. It seems likely that the graininess of the metric scale may play a role too. For instance, it is scarcely acceptable to speak of about 2 people (number of people form an integer scale) but it is quite acceptable to say about 2 volts when making a measurement with a voltmeter as fractions of volts are quite acceptable.

One wonders whether the treatment of approximatives as denoting variance is not doomed in the same way as we believe treating quantifiers as denoting numbers is. Thus Sadock (1981, p. 267) suggested a definition for *about* which was:

a sentence of the form about P is true just in case P is a quantitative proposition and there is a possible world not very different from the real world in which P is true.

Wierzbicka (1986) noted that this does not appear to differentiate *around* from *about*. She offers an analysis which does, claiming that *around* is used in a more casual way than *about*, and that *around* is used when the goal is to produce a number that is "easy to think of". With other examples she has produced formulations embodying ideas remarkably like our own conclusions for quantifiers, in that they are largely associated with higher-order interpretations. For instance, her formulation of *approximately* is:

Approximately:
if one said "it is X" it could not be more than a little different from what
is true
if it is more than X, it is not more than a little more than X
if it is less than X, it is not more than a little less than X
I say X because I want something that is easy to think of
I don't want to say something that is a little different from what is true
as if it were true

The idea here is that *approximately* implies that accuracy is possible.
In contrast, Wierzbicka sees *roughly* as implying a decision to sacrifice
precision for convenience, ease, and simplicity. Her formulation is:

Roughly:
If I say "X" it would not be more than a little different from what I want
to say
I say "X" because I want to say something that one can say
I can say something better if I spend more time thinking about it

It will be clear from these illustrations that speaker intention (and
therefore higher-order interpretation) is an integral part of the function of
these terms, in a way closely similar to what we are claiming for
quantifiers. Indeed, her analysis of the expression *at the most* (which can
form a mon dec quantifier) includes "one would think it would be more than
that". Our continuation data with the term *less than X* (p. 77) is entirely
supportive of this view. Notice that with Wierzbicka's formulation ("one
would think ... ") there is an open question as to the level(s) at which the
supposition is made.

WHERE ARE WE NOW? TASKS AND MODELS

One of our goals was to investigate what differentiates quantifiers from
one another in terms of conditions of use, and this goal is at least partly
met. Another goal was to see how the understanding of quantified
statements might fit into more general accounts of language
understanding, and of reasoning.

Reasoning

It seems to us most advisable to treat number and proportion elicitation
as an aspect of *reasoning* with quantifiers. We have already sketched out
some ideas about how such reasoning might proceed in Chapters 2 and 3.
On the basis of anecdotal evidence, it seems almost certain that not all
translations will be equally easy, and that some may even allow an

introspective protocol analysis to be used, which may provide some insights into how the more difficult decisions are made. To our knowledge, no such tests have been undertaken. To return full-circle to Chapter 1, we noted that expressions like *a significant number*, which serve as quantifiers, would explicitly invite a problem-solving approach were subjects to be invited to put numbers to them.

Because it is not easy to say precisely how many or what proportion is being denoted by nonlogical quantifiers, they appear to be poor candidates for many kinds of reasoning. For example, they do not allow valid conclusions to be drawn from standard syllogisms, although people in syllogistic reasoning tasks will sometimes treat them as though they do (Newstead et al., 1986). Because even reasoning based on the mon dec property is not deductive unless nonlogical quantifiers are given particular interpretations, we are forced to conclude that the primary function of these expressions cannot be to enable deductive reasoning. Rather, we suggest they allow for simple heuristic procedures. For instance, if I am looking for a shop that sells drinks, and I am told that *a lot of shops down the road sell drinks*, then I conclude that I am likely to be successful down the road, and that I will probably come upon a shop that sells drinks early in the sample. If the quantifier was *a few*, then I would think finding one early on in my sampling less probable; if the quantifier was *few* or *not many*, then I would certainly expect to have to sample a lot before getting a drink; it may even be the case that I won't succeed. From this plausible example, it is clear that the quantifiers concerned can lead to reasoning that has to do with probabilities, the structure of which is situation-dependent. The point is that practical, heuristic reasoning on the basis of quantified statements may be much more common than reasoning that is easily seen as syllogistic, and/or deductive.

As our hypothetical example illustrates, quantifiers might allow translation into a number of different reasoning styles. For example, the aforementioned translation is into a probabilistic mode of reasoning: How probable it is that early in walking down the street I find a shop that sells coke. But because such a way of reasoning is plausible, it does not mean that such a translation is an automatic part of understanding a quantified utterance, only that it is an optional way of reasoning. To our knowledge, there has been no study of the real-life settings in which the use of nonlogical quantifiers plays a major role.

Comprehension

Comprehension may be considered the starting point for reasoning about a statement. Thus, those issues that correspond to reasoning, described earlier, should perhaps not be thought of as part of comprehension unless a discourse makes that kind of reasoning explicit. Rather, the basic property to be captured in an account of comprehension must be the focus and inference effects. There is clearly a large amount left to do on comprehension: Our survey shows precious little here, and our own experiments perhaps provide a basis for going a little further, but no more.

Standard models of text comprehension divide broadly into two types. In the first, it is assumed that the main task of the processor is to produce a coherent representation of the text in memory. A text is assumed to be parsed into propositions, and the processor links these propositions into coherent whole (e.g. Kintsch & van Dijk, 1978; McKoon & Ratcliff, 1992). Apart from times when there seems to be a breakdown in local coherence, inferential activity is assumed to be kept to a minimum (McKoon & Ratcliff's minimalist hypothesis). The other types of account assume that the goal of the processor is to interpret the text in order to relate it to some reality that the writer or speaker is trying to portray. One example of such an account is the scenario-mapping theory of Sanford and Garrod (1981). The main assumption is that for something to be understood, it has to be related to backgroung knowledge (which they argue is organised along situation-specific lines).

Provided the step between a sentence and the representation that results is not too great, simple quantified statements may just be processed in a virtually unanalysed way. Thus (1) becomes (1'), for instance:

(1) Many people like Sally.
(1') (Many, people) & (like, people, Sally)

roughly meaning there are many people and those people like Sally. This representation does not capture the meaning of *many*, of course, leaving it as an unanalysed whole. (1') can only be the starting point of a proper interpretation. For negatives, the picture becomes more complex. For instance, following Clark (1976), *few* may be represented as a denial of *many*:

(2) Few people like Sally.
(2') (Not(many people)) & (like, people, Sally).

Thus, as long as we are not concerned with any deeper aspect of these quantifiers, it is possible to produce structures within a Kintschian framework. However, this formulation cannot capture the processes underlying some of the effects of interpretation we have explored in the earlier chapters: For instance, they have a driving effect on inference patterns, and may provide information at different levels. Such a failure is a major weakness: The proposal simply does not allow for such aspects of interpretation. Also, there is a problem with levels of interpretation, in that without going far beyond anything resembling a (text-based) proposition, it is not possible to represent levels.

An additional problem is raised by our observation that *only a few* may take its focusing properties from a direct interaction with the situation, which means that contextual access must precede (Kintschian) propositional representation. A similar point can be made on the basis of the compset data itself: Our evidence plainly shows that while some quantifiers are compset focusing, this is not a necessary property, because it does not always happen. So, if we wanted to assume that a representation like (2') could result from a sentence like (2), it would be necessary to precede this with some procedure to specify the correct instantiation.[2]

Essentially, the argument is that in order to produce a propositional representation that is not just a trivial reformulation of the sentence itself requires interpretation. Thus interpretation is more fundamental than propositional representation. None of this is new, and is certainly not peculiar to quantifiers: Sanford and Garrod (1981) made the same suggestion, preferring an explanation in which language made contact with situational knowledge at the earliest opportunity to produce a representation of the discourse (see also Garrod & Sanford, 1982). Since then a number of cases have been studied in which the use of rich situational knowledge seems to constrain representations in significant ways, including spatial prepositions (Garrod & Sanford, 1988b). For instance, what is meant by *X is on Y* depends upon the situation, as is shown by comparing *the cup is on the table* and *the fly is on the wall*. Another likely candidate for situational constraint is the interpretation of some doubly quantified sentences. Compare the following:[3]

(a) At the hotel, each room has a shower. (Rooms and showers bear a reciprocal 1:1 mapping; no many-rooms-to-single-shower mapping takes place.)

(b) At the university, each student has his or her own tutor. (A given student maps onto only one tutor, but a given tutor may map onto many students.)

It is clear that the particular representation that is appropriate for these examples depends upon the default context. So, in order to produce any kind of informative proposition, it is necessary that situational knowledge has already been invoked. We have made a similar argument in relation to the comprehension of plural anaphors (Sanford & Lockhart, 1990; Sanford & Moxey, 1991).

Focus phenomena would appear to be more readily represented in a scheme where knowledge is made differentially accessible, rather than one with a simple proposition-mapping mechanism. One possibility is to think of a comment-inducing quantifier as forcing a kind of "cognitive question" on the listener or reader. If *few X do Y*, then the question is *why do so many not do Y*, which only makes sense if there is some significance attached to what it means to do Y. So, in saying few people enjoyed the meal, the question is why, and potential answers are understood in terms of what are the requirements for enjoying a meal, and how they are sometimes blocked. Another point in favour of the situation-mapping theory is that it accounts for the evaluation of an asserted state of affairs against what is normal, which is arguably a general feature of understanding (Sanford, 1990). In order to understand that there is something strange when you hear *not many of the children liked Santa Claus*, it is necessary to access knowledge about what is the norm. Such knowledge is of course complex: It is normal for children to like Santa; it is imaginable for children not to like Santa if Santa is a store-Santa who has been drinking whisky, and so on.

Thus our preferred approach to the comprehension of quantified statements is that they predispose the system to expect certain types of subsequent input to be sensitive to specific kinds of coherence patterns. The extent to which that subsequent input is *predicted* in any detail will depend on how constrained and available the possibilities are. But if an input that does not conform to that expectation is presented, then there should be a failure in coherence, transient or otherwise. Viewed as coherence relations, the focus patterns of quantifiers also have the potential to explain why passages seem to be easier to recall when they are quantified with natural language expressions, rather than with numbers (Chapter 3). Viewed as generators of cognitive questions, quantifiers have the capacity to cause a listener to address a proposition from a particular perspective, and therefore to recruit different knowledge into reasoning.

CONCLUSION

Our review has taken us from the very simple idea that quantifiers denote proportions or numbers to one in which they are thought of having a major function of manipulating attention and patterns of inference. Of course, they do convey information about amounts, but we should not think of this as resembling a mapping onto a fine scale. These observations should come as no surprise to those who view language from a pragmatic perspective. Similarly, formal approaches to meaning have largely bypassed questions of mapping between quantifiers and numbers or proportions, and have developed broader approaches to quantification. What we have tried to do is bring together those considerations from various disciplines that might make for a more powerful approach to understanding the broad range of quantifiers in natural language. Bringing these elements together is but a start, but opens up a rich field of enquiry that has implications for a broad range of phenomena.

NOTES

1. A possible approach to scaling which might not fall foul of this problem is one in which all mon dec expressions included zero in the mapping, and in which all mon inc examples included 100%. A possible candidate is the membership function, in which the degree to which a quantifier fits a state of affairs can range over the interval $[0-1]$. It is entirely possible that some subjects might class *many X* as having a nonzero applicability index to a state of affairs where *all X* was said to be the case, so strictly speaking within a membership function, *many* could mean Z (a lower bound) or more, including *all*. But this does not seem a particularly profitable approach, because it begs the question of how people make membership judgements, and this influences their empirical establishment (we take as read that no analytic solution is possible). In fact, we suspect that when making a judgement of the applicability of *many X* to a situation where *all X* is the case, subjects' responses will be influenced by other alternatives, whether the speaker knows that *all X* is the case, and so on. If membership functions reflect mental representations, then it would be necessary for them to be fixed, regardless of these considerations.
2. It is noteworthy that any account of quantifier interpretation that includes number or fine-resolution scale-mapping is a problem for the simple propositional account because the interpretation has been shown to be context-sensitive.
3. Examples from Pieter Seuren.

References

Abelson, R. P., & Kanouse, D. E. (1966). Subjective acceptance of verbal generalizations. In S. Feldman (Ed.), *Cognitive consistency: motivational antecedents and behavioral consequents*. New York: Academic Press.

Altham, J. E. J. (1971). *The logic of plurality*. London: Methuen.

Anderson, A. H., Garrod, S. C., & Sanford, A. J. (1983). The accessibility of pronominal antecedents as a function of episode shift in narrative text. *Quarterly Journal of Experimental Psychology, 35a*, 427–440.

Ariel, M. (1990). *Accessing noun-phrase antecedents*. London: Routledge.

Barton, S. B., & Sanford, A. J. (1990). The control of attributional patterns by the focusing properties of quantifying expressions. *Journal of Semantics, 7*, 81–92.

Barwise, J., & Cooper, R. (1981). Generalized quantifiers and natural language. *Linguistics and Philosophy, 4*, 159–219.

Bass, B. M., Cascio, W. F., & O'Connor, E. J. (1974). Magnitude estimations of frequency and amount. *Journal of Applied Psychology, 59*, 313–320.

Beyth-Marom, R. (1982). How probable is probable: A numerical translation of verbal probability expressions. *Journal of Forecasting, 1*, 257–269.

Bransford, J., Barclay, J., & Franks, J. (1972). Sentence memory: A constructive versus interpretative approach. *Cognitive Psychology, 3*, pp.193–209.

Budescu, D. V., & Wallsten, T. S. (1985). Consistency in interpretation of probabilistic phrases. *Organizational Behavior and Human Decision Processes, 36*, 391–405.

Chafe, W. (1972). Discourse structure and human knowledge. In J. B. Carroll, & R. O. Freedle (Eds.), *Language comprehension and the acquisition of knowledge*. Washington DC: Winston.

Chase, C. I. (1969). Often is where you find it. *American Psychologist, 24*, 1043.

Clark, D. A. (1990). Verbal uncertainty expressions: A critical review of two decades of research. *Current Psychology: Research and Reviews, 9,* 203–235.

Clark, H. H. (1969). Linguistic processes in deductive reasoning. *Psychological Review, 76,* 387–404.

Clark, H. H. (1976). *Semantics and comprehension.* The Hague: Mouton.

Clark, H. H. (1990). Comment on Mosteller, F., & Youtz, C. "Quantifying probabilistic expressions". *Statistical Science, 5,* 2–34.

Clark, H. H. (1991). Words, the world, and their possibilities. In G. R. Lockhead, & James R. Pomerantz (Eds.), *The perception of structure: Essays in honor of Wendell R. Garner.* Washington, DC: American Psychological Association.

Clark, H. H., & Marshall, C. R. (1981). Definite reference and mutual knowledge. In A. K. Joshi, B. Webber, & I. Sag (Eds.), *Elements of discourse understanding.* Cambridge: Cambridge University Press,

Clark, H. H., & Stafford, R. A. (1969). Memory for semantic features in the verb. *Journal of Experimental Psychology, 80,* 326–334.

Cliff, N. (1957). Adverbs as multipliers. *Psychological Review, 66,* 27–44.

Cohen, J., Dearnley, E. J., & Hansel, C. E. M. (1958). A quantitative study of meaning. *The British Journal of Educational Psychology, 28,* 141–148.

Conrad, R. (1964). Acoustic confusion in immediate memory. *British Journal of Psychology, 55,* 75–84.

Doing, K. (1991). *Learning under conditions of uncertainty.* Unpublished research report, Department of Psychology, University of Glasgow.

Dolan, M. G. (1989). *Tensor manipulation networks: Connectionist and symbolic approaches to comprehension, learning, and planning.* PhD thesis, Computer Science Department, University of California at Los Angeles.

Fauconnier, G. (1979). Implication reversal in a natural language. In F. Guenther, & S. J. Schmidt (Eds.), *Formal semantics and pragmatics for natural language.* Dordrecht: Reidel.

Fox, J. (1986). Three arguments for extending the framework of probability. In *Proceedings of the the workshop on AI and decision making,* AAAI, Los Angeles, 1985. Amsterdam: Elsevier-North Holland.

Fox , J. (1991). Decision theory and autonomous systems. In M. G. Singh, & L. Trave-Massuyes (Eds.), *Decision support systems and qualitative reasoning.* Amsterdam: Elsevier-North Holland.

Garrod, S. C., & Sanford, A. J. (1982). The mental representation of discourse in a focused memory system: Implications for the interpretation of anaphoric nounphrases. *Journal of Semantics, 1,* 21–41.

Garrod, S. C., & Sanford, A. J. (1988a). Thematic subjecthood and cognitive contraints on discourse structure. *Journal of Pragmatics, 12,* 519–534.

Garrod, S.C., & Sanford, A.J. (1988b). Discourse models as interfaces between language and the spatial world. *Journal of Semantics, 6,* 147–160.

Gazdar, G. (1979). *Pragmatics.* New York: Academic Press.

Gernsbacher, M. (1990). *Language and comprehension as structure building,* Hillsdale, NJ: Lawrence Erlbaum Associates Inc.

Gernsbacher, M., Hargreaves, D., & Beeman, M. (1989). Building and accessing clausal reprentations: The advantage of first mention versus the advantage of clause recency. *Journal of Memory and Language, 28,* 735–755.

Gidron, D., Koehler, D. J., & Tversky, A. (1991). Implicit quantification of personality traits. Unpublished MS, Department of Psychology, Stanford University.

Goocher, B. E. (1965). Effects of attitude and experience on the selection of frequency adverbs. *Journal of Verbal Learning and Verbal Behavior, 4,* 193–195.

Goocher, B. E. (1969). More about often. *American Psychologist, 24,* 608–609.

Gough, P. B. (1965). Grammatical transformations and the speed of understanding. *Journal of Verbal Learning and Verbal Behavior, 4,* 107–111.

Gough, P. B. (1966). The verification of sentences: The effects of delay on evidence and sentence length. *Journal of Verbal Learning and Verbal Behavior, 5,* 492–496.

Grice, H. P. (1975). Logic and conversation. In P. Cole, & J. L. Morgan (Eds.), *Syntax and semantics,* vol. 3, *Speech acts.* New York: Seminar Press.

Grosz, B. (1977). The representation and use of focus in dialogue understanding. Technical note 15, SRI International Research Center, Stanford, CA.

Hakel, M. D. (1969). How often is often? *American Psychologist, 23,* 27–44.

Harnish , R. M. (1979). Logical form and implicature. In K. Bach, & R. M. Harnish (Eds.), *Linguistic communication and speech acts,* pp. 313–391. Cambridge, MA: MIT Press.

Hartley, J., Trueman, M., & Rogers, K. A. (1984). The effects of verbal and numerical quantifiers on questionnaire responses, *Applied Ergonomics, 11,* 149–155.

Helson, H. (1964). *Adaptation level theory.* New York: Harper & Row.

Hilton, D. J. (1985). Causal beliefs: From attribution theory to cognitive science. In J. Allwood, & E. Hjelmquist (Eds.), *Foregrounding background.* Lund (Sweden): Doxa.

Hilton, D. J. (1988). Logic and causal attribution. In D. J. Hilton (Ed.), *Contemporary science and natural explanation.* Brighton: Harvester Press.

Hilton, D. J., & Slugoski, B. R. (1986). Knowledge-based causal attribution: The abnormal conditions focus model. *Psychological Review, 93,* 75–88.

Hippler, H-J., & Schwarz, N. (1986). Not forbidding isn't allowing: The cognitive basis of the forbid–allow asymmetry. *Public Opinion Quarterly, 50,* 87–96.

Hirschberg, J. B. (1985). A theory of scalar implicature. Technical report MS-CIS-85-56, Department of Computer and Information Science, Pennsylvania State University, Philadelphia.

Holyoak, K. J., & Glass, A. L. (1978). Recognition confusions among quantifiers, *Journal of Verbal Learning and Verbal Behavior, 17,* 249–264.

Hörmann, H. (1983). The calculating listener or how many are einige, mehrere, and ein paar (some, several and a few)? In R. Bauerle, C. Schwarze, & A. von Stechow (Eds.), *Meaning, use, and interpretation of language.* Berlin: Walter de Gruyter.

Horn, L. R. (1972). *On the semantic properties of logical operators in English.* PhD thesis, University of California at Los Angeles.

Horn, L. R. (1984). Toward a new taxonomy for pragmatic inference: Q-based and R-based implicature. In D Schiffrin (Ed.), *Meaning, form, and use in context: Linguistic applications.* Washington, DC: Georgetown University Round Table 1984.

Hudson, S. B., Tannenhaus, M. K., & Dell, G. S. (1986). The effect of discourse center on the local coherence of a discourse. In C. Clifton (Ed.), *Proceedings of the eighth annual conference of the Cognitive Science Society* (pp. 96–101). Hillsdale, NJ: Lawrence Erlbaum Associates Inc.

Johnson, E. M. (1973). Numerical encoding of qualitative expressions of uncertainty. US Army Institute for the Behavioral and Social Sciences, Technical paper 150.

Johnson-Laird, P. N. (1983). *Mental models*. Cambridge: Cambridge University Press.

Johnson-Laird, P. N., & Byrne, R. (1991). *Deduction*. Hove: Lawrence Erlbaum Associates Ltd.

Jones, L. V., & Thurstone, L. L. (1955). The psychophysics of semantics: An experimental investigation. *Journal of Applied Psychology, 39*, 31–36.

Just, M. A., & Carpenter, P. A. (1971). Comprehension of negation with quantification. *Journal of Verbal Learning and Verbal Behavior, 10*, 244–253.

Kamp, H. (1984). A theory of truth and semantic representation. In T. Janssen, J Groendijk, & M. Stochof (Eds.), *Truth, interpretation, and information*. Dordrecht: Foris.

Kanouse, D. E. (1972). Verbs as implicit quantifiers. *Journal of Verbal Learning and Verbal Behavior, 11*, 141–147.

Keenan, E. L., & Stavi, J. (1986). A semantic characterization of natural language determiners, *Linguistics and Philosophy, 9*, 253–326.

Kelley, H. H. (1967). Attribution in social psychology. *Nebraska Symposium on Motivation, 15*, 192–238.

Kempson, R. M. (1975). Presupposition and the delimitation of semantics. *Cambridge Studies in Linguistics, 15*. Cambridge: Cambridge University Press.

Kintsch, W. (1974). *The representation of meaning in memory*. Hillsdale, NJ: Lawrence Erlbaum Associates Inc.

Kintsch, W., & van Dijk, T. A. (1978). Toward a model of text comprehension and production, *Psychological Review, 85*, 363–394.

Klima, E. S. (1964). Negation in English. In J. A. Fodor, & J. J. Katz (Eds.), *The structure of language*. Englewood Cliffs, NJ: Prentice-Hall.

Labov, W. (1985). Several logics of quantification. In M. Wiepokuj, M. Vauday, V. Nikiforidou, & D. Feder (Eds.), *Proceedings of the 11th Annual Meeting of the Berkeley Linguistics Society*. Berkeley, CA: Berkeley Linguistics Society.

Ladusaw, W. A. (1979). On the notion of affective in the analysis of negative polarity items. Paper presented to the 1979 Meeting of the Linguistics Society of America, Los Angeles.

Lakoff, G. (1987). *Women, fire and dangerous things*. Chicago: University of Chicago Press.

Levinson, S.C. (1983). *Pragmatics*. Cambridge: Cambridge University Press.

Marslen-Wilson, W. D., Levy, E., & Tyler, L. K. (1982). Producing interpretable discourse: The establishment and maintainance of reference. In R. J. Jarvella, & W. Klein (Eds.), *Speech, place and action*. Chichester: John Wiley.

McCawley, J. D. (1981). *Everything that linguists have always wanted to know about logic*. Oxford: Basil Blackwell.

McDonald, E. (1990). Contextual effects in quantifier interepretation: *quite a few* versus *quite a lot*. Unpublished undergraduate project, Department of Psychology, University of Glasgow.

McKoon, G., & Ratcliff, R. (1992). Inferences during reading. *Psychological Review, 99*, 440–466.

Montague, R. (1974). *Formal philosophy: Selected papers*. New Haven: Yale University Press.

Mosier, C. I. (1941). A psychometric study of meaning. *Journal of Social Psychology, 13*, 123–140.

Mostowski, A. (1957). On a generalization of quantifiers. *Fundamental Mathematics, 44*, 12–36.

Moxey, L. M. (1986). *A psychological investigation of the use and interpretation of English quantifiers.* Unpublished PhD thesis, University of Glasgow.

Moxey, L. M., & Sanford, A. J. (1987). Quantifiers and focus. *Journal of Semantics, 5*, 189–206.

Moxey, L. M., & Sanford, A. J. (1991). Context effects and the communicative functions of quantifiers: Implications for their use in attitude research. In N. Schwarz, & S. Sudman (Eds.), *Context effects in social and psychological research.* New York: Springer-Verlag.

Moxey, L. M., & Sanford, A. J. (1993). Prior expectation and the interpretation of natural language quantifiers. *European Journal of Cognitive Psychology, 5*, 73–91.

Moxey, L.M., & Sanford, A.J. (in prep.). *The acquisition of focusing properties of quantifiers.*

Moxey, L. M., Sanford, A. J., & Barton, S. B. (1990). Control of attentional focus by quantifiers. In K. J. Gilhooly, M. T. G. Keane, R. H. Logie, & G. Erdos (Eds.), *Lines of thinking*, vol 1. Chichester: Wiley.

Moxey, L. M., Sanford, A. J., & Grant, G. (in prep). Scenario characteristics and the interpretation of quantified statements.

Moxey, L. M., Sanford, A. J., & McGinley, M. T. (in prep). Quantifiers as inference generators and focus controllers.

Newstead, S. E. (1988). Quantifiers as fuzzy concepts. In T. Zetenyi (Ed.), *Fuzzy sets in psychology.* Amsterdam: Elsevier-North Holland.

Newstead, S. E., & Collis, J. M. (1987). Context and the interpretation of quantifiers of frequency. *Ergonomics, 30*, 1447–1462.

Newstead, S. E., & Griggs, R. A. (1984). Fuzzy quantifiers as an explanation of set inclusion performance. *Psychological Research, 46*, 377–388.

Newstead, S. E., Pollard, P., & Griggs, R. A. (1986). Response bias in relational reasoning. *Bulletin of the Psychonomic Society, 24*(2), 95–98.

Newstead, S. E., Pollard, P., & Reizbos, D. (1987). The effect of set size on the inter- pretation of quantifiers used in rating scales. *Applied Ergonomics, 18*, 178–182.

Parducci, A. (1968). Often is often. *American Psychologist, 23*, 828.

Pepper, S. (1981). Problems in the quantification of frequency expressions. In D. Fiske (Ed.), *New directions for methodology of social and behavioural science, 9* (pp. 25–41). San Francisco: Jossey-Bass.

Pepper, S., & Prytulak, L. S. (1974). Sometimes frequently means seldom: Context effects in the interpretations of quantitative expressions. *Journal of Research in Personality, 8*, 95–101.

Perner, J., & Garnham, A. (1989). Conditions for mutuality. *Journal of Semantics, 6*, 369–385.

Pollard, P., Service, V., & Hunter, B. (1992). Paper presented to the symposium on quantification. Second International Conference on Thinking. University of Plymouth, July 1992.

Poulton, E. C. (1968). The new psychophysics: Six models for magnitude estimation. *Psychological Bulletin, 69*, 1–19.

Poulton, E. C. (1973). Unwanted range effects from using within-subject experimental designs. *Psychological Bulletin, 80,* 113–121.

Poulton, E. C. (1989). *Bias in quantifying judgements.* Hove: Lawrence Erlbaum Associates Ltd.

Purkiss, E. (1978). *The effect of foregrounding on pronominal reference.* Undergraduate thesis, Department of Psychology, University of Glasgow.

Rapoport, A., Wallsten, T. S., & Cox, J. A. (1987). Direct and indirect scaling of membership functions of probability phrases. *Mathematical Modelling, 9,* 397–417.

Reyna, V. F. (1981). The language of possibility and probability: Effects of negation on meaning. *Memory and Cognition, 9,* 642–650.

Rothbart, M., & Park, B. (1986). On the confirmability and disconfirmability of trait concepts. *Journal of Personality and Social Psychology, 50,* 131–142.

Sadock, J. (1981). Almost. In P. Cole (Ed.), *Radical pragmatics* (pp. 257–271). New York: Academic Press.

Sanford, A.J. (1990). On the nature of text-driven inferences. In G.B. Flores d'Arcais, K. Rayner, & D. Balota (Eds.), *Comprehension processes in reading* (pp. 515–533). Hillsdale, NJ: Lawrence Erlbaum Associates Inc.

Sanford, A. J., & Garrod, S. C. (1981). *Understanding written language.* Chichester: Wiley.

Sanford, A. J., & Garrod, S. C. (1989). What, when, and how?: Questions of immediacy in anaphoric reference resolution. *Language and Cognitive Processes, 4,* 235–262.

Sanford, A.J., & Lockhart, F. (1990). Description types and method of conjoining as factors influencing plural anaphora: A confirmation study of focus. *Journal of Semantics, 7,* 365–378.

Sanford, A. J., Moar, K., & Garrod, S. C. (1988). Proper names as controllers of discourse focus. *Language and Speech, 31,* 43–56.

Sanford, A.J., & Moxey, L.M. (1991). *Notes on plural reference and the scenario mapping principle in comprehension.* Research paper HCRC RP23, Cognitive Science, University of Edinburgh.

Sanford, A. J., Moxey, L. M., & McGinley, M. (in prep.). Memory phenomena with passages containing quantifiers.

Seuren, P. A. M. (1985). *Discourse semantics.* Oxford: Blackwell.

Sharkey, N. E. (1990). A connectionist model of text comprehension. In D. A. Balota, G. B. Flores d'Arcais, & K. Rayner (Eds.), *Comprehension processes in reading,* Hillsdale, NJ: Lawrence Erlbaum Associates Inc.

Stevens, S. S. (1966). A metric for social consensus. *Science, 151,* 530–541.

Teigen, K. M. (1990). To be convincing or to be right: A question of preciseness. In K. J. Gilhooly, M. T. G. Keane, R. H. Logie, & G. Erdos. (Eds.), *Lines of thinking: Reflections on the psychology of thought.* Chichester: Wiley.

Turnbull, W. (1986). Everyday explanation: The pragmatics of puzzle resolution. *Journal for the Theory of Social Behaviour, 16,* 141–160.

Wallsten, T. S., Budescu, D. V., Rapoport, A., Zwick, R., & Forsyth, B. (1986a). Measuring the vague meanings of probability terms. *Journal of Experimental Psychology: General, 115,* 348–365.

Wallsten, T. S., Fillenbaum, S., & Cox, J. A. (1986b). Base-rate effects on the interpretations of probability and frequency expressions. *Journal of Memory and Language, 25,* 571–587.

Wason, P. C. (1965). The contexts of plausible denial. *Journal of Verbal Learning and Verbal Behavior, 4*, 7–11.

Wason, P. C., & Jones, S. (1963). Negatives: Denotation and connotation. *British Journal of Psychology, 54*, 299–307.

Weber, E. U., & Hilton, D. J. (1990). Contextual effects in the interpretations of probability words: Perceived base rate and severity of events. *Journal of Experimental Psychology: Human Perception and Performance, 16*, 781–789.

Westerståhl, D. (1989). Quantifiers in formal and natural languages. In D. Gabbay, & F. Guenthner (Eds.), *Handbook of Philosophical Logic, 4*, 1–131.

Wierzbicka, A. (1986). Precision in vagueness: The Semantics of English "approximatives". *Journal of Pragmatics, 10*, 597–614.

Zadeh, L. A. (1975). The concept of a linguistic variable and its application to approximate reasoning. III. *Information Science, 9*, 43–80.

Zimmer, A. C. (1983). Verbal versus numerical processing of subjective probabilities. In R. W. Scholz (Ed.), *Decision making under uncertainty*. Amsterdam: Elsevier-North Holland.

Zwarts, F. (1991). The syntax and semantics of negative polarity. Unpublished MS, Centre for Behavioural, Cognitive and Neurosciences, University of Groningen.

Author Index

Subject Index

Titles in the Series
Essays in Cognitive Psychology
Series Editors: Alan Baddeley, Max Coltheart, Leslie Henderson
& Phil Johnson-Laird

DEDUCTION

P.N. JOHNSON-LAIRD (Princeton University),
R.M.J. BYRNE (Trinity College, Dublin)

How do people make deductions? The orthodox answer to the question is that deductive reasoning depends on a mental logic containing formal rules of inference. The authors of this book have spent several years investigating the process. They repudiate the orthodox theory. They argue instead that people reason by imagining the relevant state of affairs, i.e. building an internal model of it, formulating a tentative conclusion based on this model, and then searching for alternative models that might refute the conclusion. Formal rules work syntactically; mental rules work semantically. The two theories therefore make different predictions about the difficulty of deductions. The book reports the results of experiments that compared these predictions in the three main domains of deduction: propositional reasoning based on connectives such as "if" and "or"; relational reasoning based on spatial descriptions; and complex reasoning based on quantifiers such as "all" and "none". In each domain, the results corroborated the model theory and ran counter to the use of formal rules.

The authors relate their findings to problems in artificial intelligence, linguistics and anthropology. They describe various computer programs based on the model theory, including one that solves a major problem in the design of electronic circuits. Finally, they show how the theory resolves a long standing controversy about the nature of rationality and whether there are cognitive universals common to all human cultures.

Contents: Logic. Deduction and Cognitive Science. Reasoning with Propositions. Conditionals. Relational Reasoning. One Quantifier at a Time: The Psychology of Syllogisms. Many Quantifiers: Reasoning with Multiple Quantification. Meta-Deduction. How to Draw Parsimonious Conclusions: An Algorithm Based on Models. Beyond Deduction: Rationality, Non - Monotonicity, and Everyday Reasoning.

ISBN 0-86377-148-3 1990 256pp. $26.95 £14.95 hbk
ISBN 0-86377-149-1 1992 256pp. $16.95 £8.95 pbk

For UK/Europe, please send orders to: *Lawrence Erlbaum Associates Ltd., Mail Order Department, 27 Church Road, Hove, East Sussex, BN3 2FA, England. Note, prices shown here are correct at time of going to press, but may change. Prices outside Europe may differ from those shown.* **Please send USA & Canadian orders to:** *Lawrence Erlbaum Associates Inc., 365 Broadway, Hillsdale, New Jersey, NJ07642, USA.*

Titles in the Series
Essays in Cognitive Psychology
Series Editors: Alan Baddeley, Max Coltheart, Leslie Henderson
& Phil Johnson-Laird

The series *Essays in Cognitive Psychology* publishes brief volumes, each of which deals with a circumscribed aspect of cognitive psychology. Taking the subject in its broadest sense, the series undertakes to encompass all topics either informed by or informing the study of mental processes and covers a wide range of subjects such as human-computer interaction, social cognition, linguistics and cognitive development as well as those subjects more normally defined as "cognitive psychology".

Berry/Dienes: Implicit Learning
0-86377-223-4 1993 208pp. $37.50 £19.95 HB

Bruce: Recognising Faces
0-86377-142-4 1989 160pp. $13.95 £8.95 PB

Evans: Bias in Human Reasoning: Causes and Consequences
0-86377-106-8 1989 160pp. $33.95 £19.95 HB / 0-86377-156-4 1990 $13.95 £8.95 PB

Eysenck: Anxiety: The Cognitive Perspective
0-86377-071-1 1992 198pp. $29.95 £19.95 HB

Frith: The Cognitive Neuropsychology of Schizophrenia
0-86377-224-2 1992 184pp. $28.50 £14.95 HB

Gathercole/Baddeley: Working Memory and Language
0-86377-265-X 1993 288pp. $46.50 £24.95 HB

Hulme/MacKenzie: Working Memory and Severe Learning Difficulties
0-86377-075-4 1992 160pp. $37.50 £19.95 HB

Johnson-Laird/Byrne: Deduction
0-86377-148-3 1991 256pp. $26.95 £14.95 HB / 0-86377-149-1 1992 $16.95 £8.95 PB

Moxey/Sanford: Communicating Quantities
0-86377-225-0 1993 144pp. $37.50 £19.95 HB

Taft: Reading & The Mental Lexicon
0-86377-110-6 1991 168pp. $37.50 £19.95 HB

Teasdale/Barnard: Affect, Cognition and Change
0-86377-079-7 1993 256pp. $46.95 £24.95 HB

Wagenaar: Paradoxes of Gambling Behaviour
0-86377-080-0 1989 120pp. Special price: $18.00 £10.00 HB

Watt: Visual Processing: Computational Psychophysical and Coginitive Research
0-86377-081-9 1987 168pp. $33.95 £19.95 HB / 0-86377-172-6 1990 $13.95 £8.95 PB

For UK/Europe, please send orders to: Lawrence Erlbaum Associates Ltd., Mail Order Department, 27 Church Road, Hove, East Sussex, BN3 2FA, England. Note, prices shown here are correct at time of going to press, but may change. Prices outside Europe may differ from those shown. Please send USA & Canadian orders to: Lawrence Erlbaum Associates Inc., 365 Broadway, Hillsdale, New Jersey, NJ07642, USA.